In gratitude to Judith Butler: for her legacy.

The performative aspects of print in the 18th century in colonial Calcutta, India.

Telling a story on print culture in colonial 18th C. Calcutta and what if it never happened?

Tapati Bharadwaj

ISBN: 9384281158
ISBN-13: 978-9384281151

WHAT IF PRINT CULTURE HAD TAKEN A DIFFERENT TRAJECTORY IN COLONIAL INDIA (POST 1780-)?

The onslaught of certain aspects of print technology in the last two decades of the 19th century in colonial Calcutta, India – initiated an epistemic shift in a manuscript-scribal realm. The socio-cultural characteristics of print – that it was more authoritative and correct/truthful than manuscripts- were also imported. But is there any ontological truth to these socially ascribed aspects of print? Is the advent of print an inevitable progression from a manuscript-scribal society?

Religious manuscripts were transferred onto printed texts and the desire was to arrive at the perfect narrative; there existed many variants of the same text and the translators would consult many editions that had been written in different time periods and collate them. What becomes evident is that there was no single authoritative text and there existed many variants of the same religious text. What would we have gained if we knew for a truth that there existed different variants of the same Hindu *shastras* and that they were altered as they were handed down over the centuries?

When religious institutions in India teach religion and Indian philosophy in the public domain and subsequently publish and disseminate these teachings, are they not cognizant and self-reflexive enough to recognise that these texts are 1) flawed as they are often and mostly collated and made up from hearsay and 2) flagrantly misogynous and embarrassingly so?

Let me clarify as to what exactly I mean by this: let us assume that a religious body teaches Saṅkhya Philosophy and has published books on this subject; the dichotomy between Puruṣa and Prakṛiti is the central motif of this philosophical system; and these characteristics are imbued with certain socially ascribed gendered attributes which are horrifyingly misogynous; such rhetoric should absolutely be banned in the public domain. There is obviously nothing ontological to Puruṣa being masculine and Prakṛiti being feminine. I quote from *The Sāṁkhya Kārikā* of Iśvara Kṛṣṇa with *The Tattva Kaumudī* of Śrī Vācaspasti Mīśra:

Verse 59: Just as a dancing girl ceases to dance after having exhibited herself to the spectators, so also, the Prakṛiti ceases to operate after having exhibited herself to Puruṣa.

Modesty here means extreme delicacy and acute sensibility of a maiden who cannot bear exposure of the prying glance of a stranger, [a "purusa"]. Similarly, the Prakṛiti, even more modest than a lady of noble birth, having once been seen by the Puruṣa through discrimination, will in no case expose herself again.

It is obvious that these religio-philosophical texts have to be rewritten and the heightened sense of misogyny erased. Purists can throw their hands up in the air – appalled at such blasphemy – but the fact is that all these religious texts, that we read as containing infallible truths, have been collated as they have been handed down over the centuries; religious theologians and philosophers – due to their ignorance and myopia - refuse to see the obvious.

Many of these religious texts were translated by the East India
Company sponsored Orientalists in the 19th century; and all these
texts have lengthy introductory comments which document the
processes that were involved. I cite a few relevant extracts from the
"Introductions" to elucidate my point: (I quote from *The Sánkhya
Aphorisms* of Kapila, with illustrative extracts from the commentaries,
translated by James R. Ballantyne, London, Trübner & Co, 1885).

The Sánkhya Aphorisms, in all the known commentaries on
them, are exhibited word for word. The variants, now given, of
the Aphorisms, afforded by accessible productions of that
character, have been drawn from the works, of which only one
has yet been printed, about to be specified:

I. The *Sánkhya-pravachana-bháshya*, by Vijnána Bhikshu. Revelant
particulars I have given elsewhere. My oldest MS. of it was
transcribed in 1654.

II. The *Kápila-sánkhya-pravachana-sútra-vṛitti*, by Aniruddha. Of
this I have consulted, besides a MS. copied in 1818, formerly the
property of Dr. Ballantyne, one which I procured to be copied,
in 1855, from an old MS. without date.

III. The *Laghhu-sánkhya-sútra-vṛitti*, by Nagesa. Of this I have two
MSS., both undated. One of them is entire; but the other is
defective by the three first Books.

IV. The *Sánkhya-pravachana-sútra-vṛitti-sára*, by Vedánti Mahádeva.
Here, again, only one of two MSS. which I possess is complete.
The other, which breaks off in the midst of the comment on
Book II., Aph. 15, is, in places, freely interpolated from No. I.
Neither of them has a date.

...

The title of the abridged form runs: "The Sánkhya
Aphorisms of Kapila, with Extracts from Vijnána

Bhiks[h]u's Commentary," &c. But this is a misrepresentation, as regards Book I., which takes up 63 pages out of the total of 175. The expository matter in that Book is derived, very largely, from other commentators than Vijnána. Vedánti Mahádeva mainly supplies it at the outset, and, towards the end, well nigh exclusively, Aniruddha. Some share of it, however, will not be traced; it having been furnished by one of Dr. Ballantyne's pandits, whom I have repeatedly seen in the very act, as by his own acknowledgment, of preparing his elucidations.

During the process of translating these religious texts in the 19th century, the Orientalist scholars referred to numerous manuscripts which often had varied connotations and these texts were collated to arrive at a final version. But we need to look carefully at the manuscripts that were referred to? – were these manuscripts that were written by the pandits and used as primary texts by the East India Company scholars – accurate? As we learn from the above extracts, "one of Dr. Ballantyne's pandits" "repeatedly" prepared his "elucidation" in an ad-hoc manner. The pandits could have made up anything and passed it off as "revealed knowledge" and no one would have been the wiser. How exactly can we gauge the nature of what is "revealed knowledge" and what are add-ons that have taken place over the centuries as they were handed down from one generation to the next.

CONTENTS

To:

Judith Butler.
for creating spaces for many generations of feminists
and for being an inspiration.

A FEW THOUGHTS.

The emergence of print in colonial Calcutta in the last two decades of the 19th century is a story that we know about. But what if the onslaught of modernity and of print – took a different trajectory? What if manuscripts were also seen as being viable modes of communication? For example, religious texts were mostly always corrupt; and when they were transferred onto print, it was deemed as a necessity that the many versions would be collated so that a final textual product would emerge. There is, thus, no definitive version of any religious text. As they were handed down over the centuries – the scribes who were also priests – would have made many changes – as they deemed needful.

The first section is an account of how print emerged in colonial Calcutta in the 1780s; the gargantuan machinery of print made its marks in the city-spaces whereby print was seen as always-forever enabling an epistemic shift away from a pre-modern, scribal society.

The second section comes up with a hypothetical proposition: what if print had not taken its trajectory and instead manuscripts were also seen as viable models within the communication circuit? Maybe – the religious texts would have been altered and the misogyny might have been erased – over the eventual passage of time.

Section I.

THE BEGINNINGS OF PRINT IN CALCUTTA. 1780-

The emergence of print culture in colonial Bengal in the last two decades of the eighteenth and early nineteenth centuries, under the East India Company, is largely an untold story. Calcutta would become the capital of the British empire, and the realm of print culture played an important role in maintaining and perpetuating British rights to this colonial territory. The history of how this realm of print culture evolved in Calcutta is central to this chapter. Ships that sailed from England carried books; printing presses were brought all the way from Europe and with the help of Indians, print workshops were set up. Many fortune seekers who traveled to India in the hope of making money through printing ventures, set up printing presses and published newspapers. Sadly, many such ventures failed. Economic losses implied the absence of a readership. The focus was, unreasonably so, on being able to use print technology even when there was no readership. Catalogues were published in Calcutta which advertised the books that had been imported from England which were auctioned on arrival like any other ships' cargoes. Printers mostly bought these imported books which were sold on to the public. Circulating libraries cropped up which needed imported books; an advertisement in the *Calcutta Gazette* in 1787 refers to the opening of a new library which stocked imported books: "Mr. Shakell [who succeeds John Hay as the printer of the *India Gazette*] having now arranged his late purchases by the last ships, and completed his Catalogue, presumes to assure the public that they will find his Circulating Library, well worthy of their patronage."[1] Tabloid-like gossip was also printed in newspapers. Oriental scholars had their works printed in Calcutta, the best known being Sir William Jones who also published journals on the proceedings of the Asiatic Society. Nonetheless, the reading public in Calcutta was small. In many ways, this realm of print enabled the community to imagine itself to be a part of the British imperialist project, and bound it with the metropolis.

---

[1] *Calcutta Gazette*, August 29, 1787.

Advertisement of a circulating library.

A Rash vow, made out of reason,
Nature abhor'd in freedom's age,
To wear the galling chains of reason.

Of wisdom's frowns soon tir'd I grew,
And sickening at pale melancholy,
To rosy joy, and frolic flew,
'Till I in time grew tir'd of folly.

Thus taught, at length my joys and cares
Now rule by turns in equal measures:
Wisdom conducts my grave affairs,
And *Levity* reigns o'er my pleasures.

H.

Answer to the ENIGMA, *in our last.*

A chest board is the fancied state
Now fill'd with men, now desolate—
Whose troops, in battle, active spread,
But sleep in peace, inert and dead.

HOMO.

NOTICE IS HEREBY GIVEN,

THAT *the Honorable Court of Directors have ordered and directed, that whenever any of their servants, Civil or Military, shall have occasion to address them, the same is to be done through the regular Channel of the Governor General and Council; addresses through any other Channel will not be attended to.*

By Order of the Right Honorable
The Governor General in Council,
JOHN WHITE, *Assist. Sec.*
Fort William, 29th August 1787.

NOTICE IS HEREBY GIVEN,

THAT *the Honorable the Court of Directors, have authorized the Period for Bond Holders, at the several Presidencies, to signify their acquiescence in the terms proposed for transferring the Indian Debt to Europe, to be extended to the 31st December 1787. In pursuance thereof, the Sub-Treasurer will receive such Bonds as are tendered to him on this account, and grant receipts in the usual mode.*

As the Honorable the Court of Directors conceive, that the advantages and security of this Remittance are not sufficiently or generally known, the Public are informed, by their order, that the Bills drawn on this account are sanctioned by the Lords Commissioners of the Treasury, in virtue of the powers vested in them by law for that purpose, and are to be charged on the general property of the Company both at home and abroad.

That the Company are pledged, in case the Bills drawn are not paid at the expiration of 548 days after date, to pay the whole within ten years from March 1790, by yearly installments of 10 per cent. That in the interim the Company are bound to pay interest on the Bills at 5 per cent. by half yearly payments, which, is a rate considerably higher than could be made in the present state of the funds on money remitted to England in any other mode. That the Company's Bonds in England bear at this time an interest of only 4 per cent. and yet are at a considerable premium. That the period of payment of these Bills was fixed, with a view of allowing for unforeseen events, which might prevent the discharge of them in a much shorter period, though the present state of the Company's affairs seems to promise it, and that the certainty, of the whole being discharged within the space above stated cannot, on any just principle, but be considered as a material advantage to the creditors.

By Order of the Right Honorable
The Governor General in Council,
J. WHITE, *Assist. Sec.*
Fort William, Aug. 29, 1787.

delivered, and in failure could under a penalty of 25 per cent to the purchaser who will be required to sign an obligation to that effect.

JOHN FARQUHAR,
Superintendant of the Powder Works,
Sept. 13th 1787.

New Library.

MR. SHAKELL having now arranged his late purchases by the last ships, and compleated his CATALOGUE, presumes to assure the public, that they will find his *Circulating Library*, well worthy of their patronage.—Catalogues will be delivered to all Subscribers, and every exertion used for their accommodation.—Mr. SHAKELL will particularly take care, that A COPY OF EVERY NEW PUBLICATION, which he has taken proper measures to be regularly supplied with, shall be reserved for the use of the Library, and from the attention which will in future be paid in conducting it, he has no doubt, in a short time, of rendering it superior to any thing of the kind before attempted in this country.

WHEREAS an Old BLACK WOOD BUREAU, the property of WARREN HASTINGS, Esq. containing amongst other things Two small Miniature Pictures, and some Private Papers, was, about the time of his departure from Bengal, either stolen from his house on the Esplanade, or by mistake sold at the Auction of his effects.

This is to give Notice,

That Mr. LARKINS and Mr. THOMPSON will pay the sum of TWO THOUSAND SICCA RUPEES to any person who shall give them such information as shall enable them to recover the contents of the Bureau.

Calcutta, Aug. 23, 1787.

[Persian/Urdu text]

جون بک عدد الماری کہنہ از چوب سیاه
مال مسٹر ہسٹین صاحب که درون آن درد
تصویر چہره مجموعه چند کاغذات بود وقت کوچ
ایشان کہ شده یا از حویلی ایشان وزدی
شده یا بوقت فروختن اجناس دیگر بغلطی
فروخته شده لہذا الحال اشتہار داده
میشود که مسٹر لارکنس صاحب و مسٹر
تامس صاحب قبول مینماید که شخصیکه
اینقدر خبر یا سراغ الماری مذکور کہ ازان خبر
کاغذ وغیره که در الماری مذکور بود توان یافت
باین صاحبان بدهد اندر هر دو صاحبان مبلغ
دو هزار روپیه سکه بان شخص خواهند داد

[Bengali text]
সাহেব ও যে জানাব সাহেব
দিউ গবহ আহাত বানমাব
ছবি ও লাগ গাওয়া আর
আহাব সাহেবগান বইহাগাব
টাকা দিন্দা দিবেন ইতি
২৭ আগস্ট ১৭৮৭ সাল

Calcutta, 1st September, 1787.

SOCIETY for the BENEFIT of SURVIVORS.

AT a General Meeting of the Subscribers, held this day at the House of Messrs. LAMBERT and Ross, the following State of the Funds was laid before them by the Secretary, and ordered to be published for the Information of the absent Members.

		Rs.		
Balance of Cash in the Chest,		10,191 10 0		
Amount of Certificates in hand as per account of particulars,				
Principal, C. Rs. 5,29,707 7 7				
Interest due on do. 20,040 3 3				
		5,49,747 10 4		
Money lent on Mort- gage,	9,280 0 0			
Interest due on do.	2,709 11 9			
		11,989 11 9		
		Current Rupees 5,71,929 00 3		

The Number of Shares subscribed being 126, the value of each Share is now 4539-1-10 Current Rupees, making an Encrease of somewhat more than 18½ per Cent. per Annum.

A. LAMBERT, Secy.

Fort St. George.

THE SUBSCRIBERS to the MADRAS COURIER in Bengal, are requested to order the amount of their subscriptions to be paid to Mr. WILLIAM MACKAY, at the HONORABLE COMPANY'S PRESS, who will grant receipts for the same, and who is authorized by the proprietors of that publication, to admit of any deductions which the Subscribers may require, from the irregularity with which they may of late have been supplied, but which will in future be carefully guarded against.

The proprietors of the COURIER flatter themselves, this request will meet with attention, as it is intended, by this means, to save the trouble of a correspondence to their Subscribers at remote stations, whose accounts are therefore made up and transmitted to Mr. MACKAY, with directions to admit such deductions as may be required, on the grounds already mentioned.

THE Creditors of the late WILLIAM JOHNSON, deceased, are requested to meet at Mr. HAMILTON's at 11 o'clock in the forenoon of the 23d September inst. to receive and take into consideration Mr. Baxter's general statement of ballances from the deceased's books, when the claims of Mr. John Shakespear, and other special matters relating to the Estate, are to be determined upon.

THE Trustees for the Creditors of Mr. WILLIAM STONE, request of those indebted to the Estate, to pay the amount of their bills to Mr. HENRY SWINBURNE, agreeable to a former notice, on or before the 15th of October next, otherwise they will be under the indispensable necessity of

By the early nineteenth century, the realm of imperial print worked contiguously with the realm of native print. There was close intimacy between the Britishers and the natives -- an intimacy that did not operate on dislike, oppression or contempt. Natives were involved in the imperial realm of print as compositors, writers, booksellers, printers, teachers and translators, mastering and replicating all aspects of print culture and technology. It was almost as if the Britishers had on display the best of their culture so that the Indians would want to emulate them – which they did. It is not an exaggeration to say that Rammohun Roy was the first native to understand what it meant to participate in the newly established English print communication circuit – by engaging with English printers, starting his own printing house, and mastering the English language and the technology of print culture.

Literary writings and journals sprung up within the realm of imperial print in the late eighteenth century, and a sphere of literary-ness was cultivated within the colonial situation. It was easy for a Britisher raised in England to arrive in India and write literary works which were meant to be read by his fellow citizens in this part of the world. What would it have taken for a native to have access to this literary realm in Calcutta and if so, how would he have been trained? Henry Derozio was the first native who was able to engage with this realm of imperial literary print that had sprung up. While at Hindu College, he would have worked alongside someone like D.L. Richardson, who was also a teacher there, besides being a poet and an editor of the *Bengal Annual* - a yearly collection of poetry and prose that was published seven times between 1830 and 1836. Richardson was an active participant in the realm of imperial literary print, and Derozio would have had access to it through him. Henry Derozio published his first collection called *Poems* in 1827; the Baptist Mission Press in Srirampur was his publishing house. The same press published one of Rammohun Roy's initial works in 1819, *A Second Conference Between an Advocate and an Opponent on the Practice of Burning Widows Alive*. Everybody in the domain of English print knew each other. It was, after all, a small realm of print. The Mission Press was run by a group of European missionaries who were deeply involved with the realm of native print, and involved in printing books that were not meant for proselytisation. Indian pandits (like Ramram Basu, Chandicharan Munshi, Rajiblochan Mukhopadhay) attached to the Baptist Mission Press also printed books of fiction in Bengali, and can thus be described as the first writers in Bengali who had their works printed. A few decades previously, this same group of pandits would have used manuscripts, but now were turning their efforts to print technology, working alongside Christian missionaries and the officials of the East India Company.

In determining the nature of this new realm of work that was established, we see that there would have been close physical contact between the Britishers and the Indians. Oftentimes, Indians worked as compositors in foundries which printed English works, without knowing the language. John Borthwick Gilchrist in his preface to *A Dictionary English and Hindoostanee*, wrote in 1798 that he was astounded with the "eternal treacherous behavior: of his Bengali assistants, a "posse of unprincipled black knaves."[2] H goes on to write about the "slavish drudgery of correcting the press … where the compositors were every one more ignorant than another of the subject they were engaged to[*sic*]."[3]A similar shift occurred in Europe, in the modern period, with the introduction of printing presses where diverse occupational groups worked with each other in the new workshops that were set up by the early printers. Elisabeth Eisenstein describes the numerous processes that were involved: "The advent of printing led to the creation of a new kind of shop structure; to a regrouping which entailed closer contacts among diversely skilled workers and encouraged new forms of cross-cultural interchange." Thus it was not uncommon to find university professors and "former priests among early printers or former abbots serving as editors or correctors," thus, coming into closer contact with metal workers and mechanics.[4] When the

---

[2] John Borthwick Gilchirst, *A Dictionary of English and Hindoostanee*. Printed by Stuart and Cooper, p. xv.

[3] Ibid, pp. xv, xii.

[4] Elizabeth Eisenstein, "Defining the Initial Shift: Some Features of Print Culture" in *The Book History Reader*, ed. David Finkelstein and Alistair McCleery (London

printing presses were introduced in Bengal, the hierarchy between the English and the Indians was maintained. The editors and the master printers were Europeans, many of whom were employed from England, while the compositors were Indians.

The development of the realm of print culture in Calcutta and its subsequent use by the natives is an interesting story; as engaging and intriguing as the development of the city itself. The exchange that took place, albeit forced, coerced and under circumstances that were far from agreeable from the perspective of the natives, can also be described as a socio-cultural and technological engagement. For example, a few of the British printers who came to Calcutta had served as apprentices in England. George Gordon was the nephew of one of the most eminent eighteenth century London printers, William Strahan, who was the King's Printer, and a friend of Samuel Johnson and Benjamin Franklin. Most of them, though, were trained in Calcutta and a few can be named: Andrew Bones, Joseph Cooper, Paul Ferris, James Hicky, Thomas Jones, James Leary, Bernard Messink, John Miller, Aaron Upjohn, Charles Wilkins.[5] Eventually, it did not matter. The Europeans settled in India and introduced certain institutions and systems of rule and governance, both for themselves and for the natives. The realm of print

and New York: Routledge, 2002), pp. 156-157.

[5] For more see Graham Shaw, *Printing in Calcutta to 1800*, pp. 42-71.

was one such institution. Gradually, the Indians learnt it, and replicated all aspects of print. This process of cultural transmission and exchange did not pass through any phase of mimicry. What did matter was that the realm of print allowed both Britishers and the natives to engage with each other and for the natives, to reach out to a global readership.

INSTITUTIONALISING PRINT: GRAMMAR BOOKS.

Nathaniel Halhed's *A Grammar of the Bengal Language* (1778) has reasons to be lauded as the first in many ways: most importantly, it was multilingual, involving the efforts of both the English and the natives.[6] For the natives, living within a manuscript culture, to see printed texts emerge, transcribing and documenting Bengali words and their English synonyms, would have been a unique experience. The book was printed in Hooghly, made its way to England and was sold in London by Elmsley. In 1783, a review in an English journal, *The English Review*, succinctly pointed to the numerous aspects of ingenuity in the book:[7]

---

[6] Nathaniel Brassey Halhed, *A Grammar of the Bengal Language*. 1778. Reprint, ed. R. C. Alston (England: The Scolar Press, 1969).

[7] Review of "A Grammar of the Bengal Language," *The English Review, or, An Abstract of*

The work now before us (the first perhaps printed in Hindostan) has many circumstances of novelty, as well as of utility to recommend it to public attention. One gentleman presents us with the elements of a language hitherto disregarded, and almost unknown in Europe. Another gentleman employs the extraordinary efforts of a singular and persevering genius in the fabrication of types of a very novel and difficult construction: while we find a Governor General, (unlike every description of public men in Britain) amidst all the busy scenes of war and state affairs, cultivating the arts of peace; advising, soliciting, animating men of ability to undertake, to persevere, and to accomplish pursuits so laudable in themselves, and so strongly pointed to attest and extend the India Company's most essential interests in Bengal.[8]

The review drew upon an easy equation between the study of Indian languages and its use in maintaining the British empire in India. The argument that was made was an interesting one: the aim of the British government was "to establish an empire over the minds as well as over the country of the natives," and grammar books were needed to allow for an "easy" intercourse with the "native" as no people could "cheerfully submit to rulers" they did not

---

English and Foreign Literature Vol. I (1783): 5-14.

[8] Ibid., p. 12. Print actually began in 'Hindostan' in 1556 when the Jesuits established the first printing press in Goa.

understand."[9] The central assumption within eighteenth century British print culture, where print technology was seen at the apex of communication forms, was transferred onto the colonies by the East India Company. Such was the realm of print that evolved in Calcutta in the last two decades of the twentieth century to serve the needs of the empire.

The realm of print was a complicit partner in the processes of empire making. When we consider how print was intrinsic to the formation of a colony by the East India Company, we are given a different perspective on the nature of how print entered India. In *Indian Ink, Script and Print in the Making of the English East India Company*,[10] Miles Ogborn looks at the importance of different modes of writing to the English East India Company in the seventeenth and eighteenth centuries, arguing that the company's world was "one made on paper as well as on land and sea."[11] Central to the book is the assumption that the "complexities of the exertion of power and the making of knowledge and profit in these mercantile and imperial worlds" are made evident in how different forms of writing

[9] Ibid., p. 5.

[10] Miles Ogborn, *India Ink, Script and Print in the making of the English East India Company* (Chicago: University of Chicago Press, 1997).

[11] Ibid., p. xvii. What Ogborn wants to demonstrate is a way to look at the interconnections between imperial spaces, knowledge and power through "recent histories of reading, writing, and publishing." He goes on to argue that the operations and workings of power are found in the "concrete processes of the making, distribution, and use of texts as material objects." (pp. 5-6).

were developed and deployed by the Company; thereby examining these texts can give us an insight in the connections between power and knowledge.[12]

For example, the correspondence of Robert Boyle,[13] the scientist who was also a member of the Court of Committees that managed the Company's operations, reveals that his world was also the "world of the English East India Company."[14] The leading scientific figures of England were involved in the processes of empire making (despite denying their monetary involvements), thus shifting the dynamics of how colonization took place – it was not a mere event of brutal force and gunpowder but the intellectual elite of England were involved and seemingly quite keen to disseminate knowledge.

---

[12] Ibid., p. xxi.

[13] Robert Boyle owned East India stocks, and used his position in the Company to find jobs for those who used his patronage.

[14] Ibid., p. xvii. Boyle, though, was keen to emphasis that his involvement with the company was out of the desire for knowledge and not profit. Ogborn writes that historians of science consider Boyle's involvement in the seventeenth century scientific revolution and the foundation of the Royal Society to argue for a "conception of scientific knowledge that understands it as an engagement with political concerns that are inseparable from matters of practice." p.xxi.

PROCESSES OF STANDARDIZATION

The use of print in the colonies was not inevitable as manuscripts were used as well as handwritten notices and circulars. Initially print was seen as a threat and many printers who attempted to print were deported to Europe. The works of Orientalist scholars are well known, but what need was there for grammar books and dictionaries to be printed and publicized and what part did the dissemination of printed material play in the debate of empire building in Bengal? Government patronage did determine the nature of print in the early years and for the publication of works on philology and grammar.[15] Patterns of dissemination and distribution were also determined by government finance.[16] Printed texts were circulated, enabling an imperial sphere

---

[15] Ibid., p. 220.

[16] Ibid., p. 221.

of 'social communication' to be constructed that included readers and writers in India and in England, but this cannot necessarily be assumed to be a "consensual interpretative community"[17] for natives were not equal collaborators in this enterprise. These grammar books, legal texts and translations of religious texts were printed, placing them within an "imperial circuit" of production, dissemination and reception.[18] Moreover, the needs of empire building determined why grammar books were printed, and did not necessarily reflect the needs of the natives. Subsequently, these grammar books – meant to aid in standardizing Indian languages -- did become the definitive norm in India.

When examining the nature of how grammar books emerged in Calcutta, written on the same lines as grammar books in England, and the complicated logic behind them, it would be relevant to understand how grammar books evolved in England in a completely different context – or for that matter, how the emergence of the printing press helped in standardizing the English language. When William Caxton set up his printing press around 1476, it was about fifty years since the Chancery English had been adopted as the standard, based on the London and the East Midland dialect. Caxton's press aided in making this dialect of English as the norm. Caxton set up his printing press in Westminister close to Parliament, and decided to print in

---

[17] Ibid., p. 223.

[18] Ibid., p. 225.

the vernacular, realizing the economic prospects of the new venture. This was a smart move, as there had been other printers who had set up presses on Oxford and St. Albans, and had failed. These printers had published academic books in Latin, not realizing that such books could easily be available through trade with the Continent.[19]

It was largely for economic reasons that Caxton was searching for a "relatively stable language variety that could serve a superregional function to speakers of different dialects."[20] He used a dialect that was the most widely accepted written variety, and used by the literate segments of society, which constituted his own intended audience. By the end of the fifteenth century, "economic motivations contributed significantly to earlier linguistic and political ones in the standardization of the language."[21] Writing dictionaries and grammar books were some of the processes that were involved in standardizing a language. The first dictionaries were written in the early eighteenth century and were meant to include new, unfamiliar words that had entered the English language over the centuries; dictionaries were needed to explain these words to the common user or to the well educated[22] and did not include those words that were in everyday use. Nathan Bailey's

[19] Norman Blake, *Caxton and his World* (London: Andre Deutsch,1969).

[20] Terttu Nevalainen and Ingrid Tieken-Boon van Ostade. "Standardisation," in *A History of the English Language*. eds. Richard Hogg and David Denison (Cambridge: Cambridge University Press, 1992), pp. 271-311; p. 278.

[21] Ibid., p. 278.

[22] Ibid., p. 283.

Dictionarium Britannicum, that was written in 1730, was the first dictionary to include all words and was subsequently used as a source for Johnson's *Dictionary of the English Language* (1755).[23] Early grammarians resorted to Latin grammar to provide them with a model and English grammar was not considered as an object worthy of study for its own sake till 1653 with the publication of Wallis's *Grammatica Linguae Anglicanae*. English grammar was treated like Latin, and emphasis was given to its morphology. Grammarians of the eighteenth century wanted to fix the language, only to realize that a living language could not be fixed. Lindley Murray's grammar book (first published in 1795) came to be looked upon as a handbook of English grammar. English grammar books were taken as a model for grammar books on native languages and the need to write such books were driven by the needs of empire and the East India Company.

The nature of how these grammar books in the colonial context came to be written is symptomatic of Tony Ballantyne's argument that imperial knowledge was often disembodied from the socio-traditional context from within which they emerged. Ballantyne argues that colonial states gathered knowledge from a wide range of sources about the colonies and printing was crucial to the systematization and dissemination of colonial knowledge.[24]

---

[23] Ibid., p. 284.

[24] Tony Ballantyne, "What Difference does Colonialism Make? Reassessing Print and Social Change in an age of global imperialism," in *Agent of Change: Print Culture Studies After Elizabeth*

This form of codified knowledge was the basis of the day to day operation of colonial power, but "the processes by which they were created profoundly altered the knowledge they recorded, disembodying these traditions, wrenching them free of the traditional social contexts of knowledge transmissions to revalue them as an aid to the operation of imperial authority."[25] Recent histories of empire look at the connections between the role of colonial knowledge and the establishment of colonial authority.[26]

Even as colonial authorities used print to exercise power, what is not very clear is the nature of power? It is easy to write off colonial power as being absolute but power in this instance – as the preceding analysis has shown – was far from being totalitarian. Colonial authority did not operate in a binary of absolute coercion and pliant submission and the natives – for that matter, the intellectual elites in many instances – participated in the dissemination of colonial authority. Those who were being ruled allowed themselves to be a part of this process of technological exchange, even as it was used to make them subordinates.

L *Eisenstein*, eds. Sabrina Baron, Eric Lindquist and Eleanor Shevlin (Amherst: University of Massachusetts Press, 2007).

[25] Ibid., p. 345.

[26] As printing was "central" to the working of the modern colonial state, it has "become an important point of debate in the scholarship on modern empire building"; print was an important tool for "colonial administrators, missionaries and social reformers" and was reconceptualized in the colonial situation. Ibid., p. 343.

REALMS OF POWER

A basic fundamental question that keeps on arising over and over again is on how the realm of print in colonial Bengal (between 1780 and 1800) perpetuated and embodied power? Was it such a simple process of shifting ship loads of people and technology across the oceans and settling them down in Calcutta? What was it that motivated people to move themselves from England, apart from the obvious monetary attraction? Examining a few moments (and a few people involved) in the process of technological exchange will allow us a more nuanced understanding of what is usually written off as mere mimicry by most postcolonial theorists.

George Gordon was one of the printers who came and started a printing press in Calcutta; he was also the only printer who was professionally trained as a printer before his departure from England.[27] Gordon was the nephew of one of the most eminent eighteenth century London printers, William Strahan, who was also the king's printer, and a friend of Samuel Johnson and Benjamin Franklin. He was recommended by his uncle to the Court of Directors of the East India Company and was the only licensed printer by the Company. Another well known printer was Charles Wilkins who joined the East India Company in 1770 as a writer; he was well versed in Persian and Bengali and made the earliest known types in Bengali.[28] He was also invited to establish a printing press for the Company so that it could print its own official documents. He was appointed as the first superintendent of the Honourable Company's Press in December 1778. The press was in Malda where the Company's factories were located, and Wilkins was also the supervisor of these factories. Here Wilkins made a set of Persian types. The Company's press was removed to Calcutta in 1781 where Wilkins was transferred as the Persian and Bengali translator to the Committee of Revenue. The first work to be printed here was his own *A Translation of a royal grant of land by one of the ancient Rajaas of Hindostan*; Francis Gladwin's translation of *Ayeen Akbari* was the last work to be printed under his supervision in 1783. After Wilkins left for Benaras in December 1783, Gladwin succeeded him as the

---

[27] For more see Graham Shaw, *Printing in Calcutta before 1800* (Oxford: Oxford University Press, 1981), pp. 48-50.

[28] For more see Shaw, pp. 69-71.

superintendent of the press in January of 1784. All of these people were involved in the process of empire making, meticulously learning the languages and the habits of the natives. Some of them carried with them the best of British civilization and imparted it to the natives.

It would therefore be a more meaningful discussion if we understood power as operating in a more sophisticated manner rather than simply being imposed upon others in a binary fashion. Those Britishers who traveled to India were people who were part and parcel of the Juggernaut of empire making and they were blood and flesh people and not necessarily heinously mean or cruel. The intellectual brahminical elite allowed themselves to be participants in this process, only because they were involved in a new epistemic shift; the tradeoff must have been fair. It is rather simplistic to construe the natives as being overpowered or incapable of resistance of any sort. The sheer fascination with the new-ness of the social and technological aspects of print culture might have been, after all, irresistible.

CAPTURING NATIVE PRINT AND EMPIRE MAKING

It is slightly ironic that the first book to be printed in Bengal, India, Nathaniel Halhed's *A Grammar of the Bengal Language* (1778), was under the patronage of the East India Company and meant for a British readership.[29] The book was printed in Hooghly, made its way to England and sold in London by Elmsley. In 1783, a review in an English journal, *A New Review*, described the book as "classical" and of much use to those Britishers who traveled to India to work in "public departments," allowing for better "correspondence" between the natives and the rulers.[30] The

---

[29] Nathaniel Brassey Halhed, *A Grammar of the Bengal Language*. Hooghly in Bengal, 1778. Reprint. ed. R. C. Alston (Menston, England: Scolar Press, 1969).

[30] "Review of *A Grammar of the Bengal Language*," *A New Review* 3(1783): 156-157.

need for communication was but one of the reasons why the book was praised; the Bengali "characters" are "beautiful," the reviewer wrote, and would arouse the curiosity of the British reader. Letterpress technology had captured the "exotic" beauty of the Bengali script, revealing the apparent mastery of western print mechanization over scribal manuscripts. The central assumption within eighteenth century British print culture, where print technology was seen at the apex of communication forms, was transferred to the colonies by the East India Company. Such was the realm of early print that evolved in Calcutta, in the last two decades of the eighteenth century, serving the needs of the empire.

Here, I look at the "communications circuit" in the early phases of print culture in Calcutta, that is pre-1800, and how it catered to the specific needs of the Britishers. The booksellers, writers and printers were English. That is, prior to the turn of the century, the realm of print culture was a closed circuit—all books, newspapers, gazettes, legal translations, in fact, all printed material had a very specific readership and catered to the practical, aesthetic and intellectual needs of the Europeans. Interestingly enough, the newspapers also occasionally had news items in native languages. One wonders, who would have been the readers of news in Bengali in a newspaper that catered to the Britishers? Would the English readers be expected to know enough of the language, barely nine years after Halhed's Bengali grammar book was published? I have mentioned earlier that as the grammar book was meant to both educate those Britishers who traveled to India for work, and also to impress the non-native readers about the beauty of the Bengali fonts, the multilingual newspaper was printed on similar lines. The polyphonic nature of the newspaper at this early stage of print in colonial Calcutta is remarkable.

I examine the nature of the "communications circuit" that evolved in Calcutta, drawing attention to the interrelationship between technology, print culture and imperial knowledge-making and the motives behind how the "circuit" of printers and writers operated. The realm of print culture in Bengal was defined by the imperatives of empire; it would not have emerged the way it did if it had not been for the economic support of the East India Company. To clarify what I mean by imperial print, I examine the works of Sir William Jones and the Company Orientalists, a body of scholarship that emerged under the auspices of the East India Company. For Sir William Jones, steeped in the culture of print, the technology of print had the power to transform a pre-modern, Indian scribal culture into western modernity.

The power of this realm of print culture is evident in the fact that it enabled to maintain control over the colonial territories. As early as 1783, a review appeared in an English journal, which when describing the need for grammar books and language books on the natives said that "without an easy and general intercourse with the natives, through the medium of language, no system of regulation … can promote any solid, rational or permanent establishment of authority and power" as no people could "cheerfully submit to rulers" they did not understand."[31] More importantly, the cultivation of this kind of imperial print was a sustained effort and in keeping with the East India Company policies; the Company's trading success was a result of the scientific revolution of the seventeenth century and the EIC had eminent scientists of the Royal Society, like Robert Boyle, Isaac Newton, Joseph Banks as its directors or major shareholders. Not surprisingly, Company Orientalism had a small but influential readership, a sphere of print communication that informed the practices of empire formation. The body of Orientalist work that emerged from India in the late eighteenth century and influenced European notions of the colonies was a result of print capital. The works of the Calcutta based Orientalists were widely disseminated in Europe as a result of Jones' letter writing and print culture.[32] The "communications circuit" was immense, spreading across continents. A single author, located in India, had books printed in India and England and these were translated and read by a European audience.

---

[31] "Review of Halhed's Grammar Book," *The English Review, or, An Abstract of English and Foreign Literature* 1(1783): 5-14, 5.

[32] Ballantyne, *Orientalism and Race*, pp. 1-55.

The characteristics of Western print.

Empire making was made possible through the realm of print culture. Not only was the technology transferred, but so were the socially ascribed characteristics of print. Sir William Jones, operating within the ideology of eighteenth century print culture that associated print with truth, assumed that the technology of print had the power to transform a pre-modern, Indian scribal culture into western modernity. But this equation between print and truth was not intrinsic to letterpress technology as till the early decades of the eighteenth century there was a suspicion of the printed word. In *The Nature of the Book: Print and Knowledge in the Making*, Adrian Johns draws attention to assumptions about print culture, stating that what we "often regard as essential elements and necessary concomitants of print are in fact rather more contingent than generally acknowledged. Veracity in particular is … extrinsic to the press itself, and has had to be grafted onto it."[33] A printed book could never be trusted to be what it claimed. Johns claims that in the seventeenth century, piracy and plagiarism were dominant fears. It was a matter of routine that books could be considered dubious; therefore, it was impossible to trust any printed report. Pirate editions of Shakespeare, Donne and Sir Thomas Browne were liable to egregious errors, and so was Sir Isaac Newton's unauthorized publication of *Principia* and the first

---

[33] Adrian Johns, *The Nature of the Book: Print and Knowledge in the Making* (Chicago: University of Chicago Press, 2000), p. 2.

scientific journal, the *Philosophical Transactions*. It was only in 1760 that the first book was printed without any errors.

Not surprisingly, till early in the eighteenth century, print was seen as suspect, without any intrinsic characteristic of truth. Printers, booksellers and authors, who gained the most commercially, put forward the notion of the truth and superiority of print in contrast to manuscripts. If print culture was to be a viable economical institution, a "communications circuit" involving the author, publisher, the printer, the shipper, the book-seller, and the reader had to be in harmonious coexistence, with the reader believing in the veracity of print. Writers were often propagandists of print, as much as theorists, and this is how Paula McDowell describes Daniel Defoe, the eighteenth century's "most prolific printed author," who wrote in his *Essay upon Literature* (1726), "The Printing Art has out-run the Pen, and may pass for the greatest improvement of its Kind in the World."[34] All of Defoe's writings imply that the oral past should be, but is not, cut off from the print-oriented present and future. Regarding Defoe's historical fiction, *A Journal of the Plague Year* (1772), McDowell points out that the text moves diachronically in time as the present modern age of print was a move away from the backward past associated with oral culture. Defoe also moves "synchronically across different communicative modes that in reality are coexisting and interdependent"

---

[34] Paula McDowell, "Defoe and the Contagion of the Oral: Modeling Media Shift in A Journal of the Plague Year," *PMLA* 121(1): 87-106.

but are represented as parts of a "linear, progressive development."[35] Defoe's printed books contribute to an "emergent model of a hierarchy of forms of communication with print at its apex"[36] as the writer attempts to draw an equation, not existing before, between print and "enhanced fidelity, reliability, and truth."[37] In this process, orality is relegated to the realm of old wives tales.

By the time of Sir William Jones, England had become an increasingly print-oriented society, shifting away from its oral past. This explains Jones' feverish desire to transcribe every manuscript into print, as the process would lend an element of fixity to unstable scribal texts. In an advertisement in *The Calcutta Gazette*, in 1789, Sir William Jones wrote:

> The correctness of modern Arabian and
> Persian Books is truly deplorable, nothing can
> preserve them in any degree of accuracy but
> the art of printing; and if Asiatic literature
> should ever be general, it must diffuse itself,
> as Greek learning was diffused in Italy after
> the taking of Constantinople, by mere
> impressions of the best manuscripts without
> versions or comments, which future scholars

---

[35] Ibid., p. 88.

[36] Ibid., p. 89.

[37] Johns, *The Nature of the Book*, p. 5.

would add at their leisure to future editions:
but no printer should engage in so expensive a
business without the patronage and the purse
of monarchs of states, or society of wealthy
individuals or at least without a large public
subscription.[38]

Jones was extremely conscious of entering a realm of
scribal culture in Bengal, and this is reflected in his desire
to constantly transfer manuscripts into printed texts. In a
way, by transferring written texts into print, his central aim
was to codify knowledge, and in the process allow for
control of what was disseminated about India. In 1768,
before Jones sailed for India, he wrote to Count Revicski,
the Imperial Minister of Warsaw, describing the difficulties
that were present when trying to locate a single meaning in
manuscripts; it was "impossible to find two manuscripts [of
Oriental literature] without error," he wrote, and "it was
"absolutely necessary … to possess two copies of every
one" which he would read so that "faults of the one"
would be "corrected by the other."[39] In many of his letters,
Jones voices a similar concern, where he reveals an intense
desire to transcribe everything that he reads into print.
Writing to one Dr. Patrick Russel in 1786, he said, "I
congratulate you on the completion of your two works, but
exhort you to publish them."[40] Jones goes on to say, "think

---

[38] William Jones, *The Calcutta Gazette*, October 29, 1789.

[39] Jones, *Complete Works, Vol. 1*, p. 101.

[40] Jones, *Complete Works, Vol. 2*, p. 99.

how much fame Koenig lost by delaying his publications"
and even if printing is "dear at Calcutta," if "government"
printed Russel's works, he would "cheerfully superintend
commas and colons."[41] A year later, Jones voices a similar
concern in another letter,

> I have just read a very old book on that art [of
> music] in Sanskrit. I hope to present the world with
> the substance of it, as soon as the transactions of
> our society [The Asiatic Society] can be printed; but
> we go slowly, since the press is often engaged by
> government; … The *Asiatik Miscellany*, to which you
> allude, is not the publication of our society, who
> mean to print no scraps, nor any *mere* translations. It
> was the undertaking of a private gentleman, and will
> certainly be of use in diffusing Oriental literature,
> though it has [not?] been so correctly printed as I
> could wish.[42]

Manuscripts are seen as being less than perfect while
printed texts allow for true, correct knowledge to emerge.
Print technology is invested with a kind of truth power that
is denied to manuscripts. Power resides in the capacity to
be able to use print, and in the process, to make it
accessible to larger groups of people. Mechanical
reproducibility, made possible as a result of letterpress

---

[41] Ibid., pp. 100-101.

[42] Ibid., pp. 123-124.

technology, would make knowledge more reproducible but also more authentic. The realm of print spread across continents, and made it possible to control the colonial territories.

The East India Company was interested in documenting all forms of knowledge that it could lay its hands on and supported many such works; all grammar books and translations were justified as they could help in empire building. Translations of historical and administrative works were seen as essential in carrying out the operations of the Company, and often, these works were partially subscribed and recommended by the East India Company. For example, Francis Gladwin's translation of Abu al-Fazl Ibn Mubarak's *Ayeen Akbery* was published in 1783, and seen as an endeavor that would serve the company as the "work comprehends the original constitution of the Mogul Empire, described under the immediate inspection of its founder; and will serve to assist the judgment of the Court of Directors."[43] In the introduction to the translation, there is a lengthy explanation of how the text would be beneficial to the company: "It will show where the measures of their administration approach to the first principles, which perhaps will be found superior to any that have been built on their ruins, and certainly most easy, as the most familiar to the minds of the people, and when any deviation from

---

[43] *Ayeen Akbery: or The Institutes of the Emperor Akber, Vol. I.* trans. by Francis Gladwin, pp. xi-xii. 1783.

them may be likely to counteract, or to assimilate with them."[44] The third volume contained a "full account of the religion of the Hindoos; their books and the subjects of them: their several sects and the points in which they differ."[45] There were astronomical notes which were provided by Reuben Burrow, who applied with "great diligence to the study of the Sanskrit language" and also made a "perfect knowledge of Hindoo astronomy."[46] The Governor General and Council recommended to the Court of Director the purchase of one hundred and fifty copies of the first edition of the *Ayeen Akbery*; this was, after all, a "work which may prove of the utmost utility to the Company, as it contains the original Institutes of the Sultan Akber, the founder of the empire."[47] Company patronage did provide a much needed monetary impetus for native types to be developed and these were subsequently used by the natives.

---

[44] Ibid., p. xi-xii.

[45] The "Preface" to *Ayeen Akbery, Vol. III.* trans. by Francis Gladwin. Printed by William Mackay, Calcutta Gazette Press, 1786.

[46] Ibid.

[47] *Fort William-India House Correspondence, vol. IX, 1782-85*, edited by B.A. Saletore, Delhi, 1959. Also Gladwin's "Preface" to *Ayeen Akbery, Vol. II*, p. iii.

GRAMMAR BOOKS AND IMPERIAL RULE

Grammar Books and print culture

Nathaniel Halhed's *A Grammar of the Bengal Language* defines 1778, the year of its publication, as a watershed moment in the history of print as it entrenches British colonial print culture in Calcutta and the text is transparent about its motives and origins. Halhed has to be seen as working within the existing ideological notions of empire making, where Britain defined itself as civilized and modern by characterizing India and its languages as primitive. The author-grammarian draws attention to the mechanical aspects of print technology; the natives are emasculated and deviant, awaiting British colonization for progress, and in a similar manner, archaic Indian scribal culture would undergo modern change through print technology. In order to maintain order and control the colonies, it was essential to learn the languages of the Indians—the underlying assumption was that the territorial domain of the colonies could be managed through the realm of print.

Grammar books on Indian languages were meant to aid the East India Company. In order to maintain order in the colonies, it was essential to learn the languages of the Indians; this territorial domain of the colonies could be controlled by mastering the realm of native languages and codifying them in grammar books. Grammar books like Francis Gladwin's *The Persian Moonshe* (1795), *A Vocabulary, Persian, Arabic, and English* (1797), which aided the British to learn Persian and Bengali, were printed by English printing presses to cater to the needs of the administrators of the Company. This realm of texts was specific to the English community in Calcutta, and was meant to aid in trade and rule. Such texts play a similar role as that of colonial cartography in the processes of British empire building. As Ian Barrow argues, the mapping of India and the creation of colonial territory helped to build British national identity.[48] Colonial cartography depicted histories of British territorial possession and these histories helped the British to remake themselves as legitimate rulers while also reinforcing the notion of a British national identity. Grammar books, for the most, made colonial possession more legitimate. One of the first books to be written was

---

[48] Ian Barrow, *Making History, Drawing Territory. British Mapping in India, c. 1756-1905* (New Delhi: Oxford University Press, 2003).

Nathaniel Halhed's *A Grammar of the Bengal Language*, in 1778. In 1783, a reviewer in *The English Review* wrote that the "settlements in the East" deserve the "chief attention" of Britain. A printed grammar book would draw public attention to the language spoken by "millions of industrious British subjects" and would also aid in the "proper management of the commercial, military and revenue departments in Bengal."[49]

Printing a grammar book would allow for better communication between the government and the natives, enabling benevolent rule. Print was an extension of the state and the state defined itself through print. For Halhed:

> The wisdom of the British Parliament has within these few years taken a decisive part in the internal policy and civil administration of its Asiatic territories…. Much however still remains for the completion of this grand work; and we may reasonably presume, that one of its most important desiderata is the cultivation of a right understanding and of a general medium of intercourse between Government, and its subjects; between the natives of Europe who are to rule, and the Inhabitants of India who are to obey.[50]

---

[49] "Review of Halhed's *A Grammar of the Bengal Language*", *The English Review*, p. 5-14.

[50] Halhed, *A Grammar*, pp. i-ii

If the British were to rule, then print would play an important function in making that rule possible. Halhed draws a comparison between the present British conquest of Bengal and the colonial desire to learn the language of the natives with a historical antecedent, when the Romans, " a people of little learning and less taste, [who] had no sooner conquered Greece than they applied themselves to the study of Greek."[51] Learning the language of Bengal would allow the rulers to explain the benevolent principles of that Legislation whose decrees they enforce[d]"; the desire was to "convince" and persuade the natives" while they commanded.[52] The economic imperatives were enormous and would be no less beneficial to the Revenue Department.[53] In all respects, the printed grammar book was a means of inevitable social progress in the colonies.

Territorial control was possible because of the scientific and technological advancement of England. A similar argument is made in *Mapping an Empire: The Geographical Construction of British India, 1765-1843*, where Matthew Edney argues that that the extensive trigonometrical surveys conducted in southern and central India in the nineteenth century encouraged many Britishers to believe that they knew the real India.[54] Trigonometrical

---

[51] Ibid., p. 1.

[52] Ibid., pp. i-ii.

[53] Ibid., p. xv.

[54] Matthew Edney, *Mapping an Empire. The Geographical Construction of British India, 1765-1843*

surveys had the power to depict land in a precise manner and the ideal of scientific, rational depiction was a contrast to the ineffectual and non-rational Indians and the non-elite sections of British society who were caricatured as ineffectual and not capable of sustained rational thought. The power of trigonometrical mapping, with its seemingly objective and scientific nature, permitted the British administrators to believe that these cartographic portrayals could capture the real India, and demonstrate the superiority of the British. The maps portrayed more than land; they depicted totalizing power and knowledge. The belief behind print technology was that the Western disciplinary institutions could control the colonies.

(Chicago: University of Chicago Press, 1999).

MOVING AWAY FROM A SCRIBAL CULTURE

By the latter part of the eighteenth century, print culture was seen as being superior to other forms of communication. The move was towards codifying into print all the existing knowledge systems documented in a scribal-manuscript culture and this was construed as a shift into inevitable progress. Halhed draws attention to the mechanical aspects of print technology. The book, he writes, was to be seen as "extraordinary" and an "instance of mechanic abilities" and meant for the British public whose "curiosity" would be "strongly excited by the beautiful characters" that were displayed in the text.[55] Making Bengali fonts was not easy as the Bengali letters were "very difficult to be imitated in steel." Halhed

---

[55] Halhed, *A Grammar*, p. xxiii.

erroneously credits Mr. Wilkins, an employee of the East India Company as being successful by undertaking the various occupations of "Metallurgist, the Engraver, the Founder and the Printer,"[56] and completely misrepresents the fact that natives were also involved; in fact, Panchanan Karmakar played an important role along with Wilkins. The process that was involved, of creating types in steel, of transferring and establishing clarity to the illegible, handwritten manuscripts—where the "inaccuracy of their writings" frequently deviated from their original forms— imparted a sense of authenticity and fixity to the act of writing.[57] Technology is celebrated as it has the capacity to represent even the most difficult of languages. Print technology made pure the existing state of social affairs; the various "impositions and forgeries with which Bengal at present abounds," Halhed wrote, would be done away with.[58]

Halhed has to be seen as working within the existing ideological notions of empire-making. Britain defined itself as civilized and modern by characterizing India and its languages as primitive. British rule was conceived as benevolent, a system of government, made possible and facilitated through print unlike scribal culture. The British nation was interested in "marking the progress of her

---

[56] Ibid., p. xxiv.

[57] Ibid., p .3.

[58] Ibid., p. xxiv.

conquests by a liberal communication of Arts and Sciences, rather than by the effusion of blood."[59] The "poorer classes of people" were oppressed in a "country still fluctuating between the relics of former despotic dominion, and the liberal spirit of its present legislature."[60] To "enforce stability" in the British empire and in order for the administration to gain in "popularity," the "discouraged husbandman, the neglected artist, and oppressed laborer" would seek "asylum" in British "territories."[61] Print technology possessed all the rational and benevolent characteristics of the English government; the "vigour" and "impartiality" that marked the operations of the government were seen in the printed grammar book. Moreover, Halhed defines how the Bengali language was to be, and attempts to cleanse it, by doing away with "foreign" influences[62] and by presenting the Bengali language as "derived from its parent the Sanskrit";[63] words that were not "natives of the country are not a part of his text and he has only selected the "most authentic and ancient compositions."[64] The study of the language, Halhed argued, was made difficult due to the "carelessness and ignorance of the people"; it had many "anomalous

---

[59] Ibid., p. xxv.

[60] Ibid., p. xvi.

[61] Ibid., p. xvi.

[62] Ibid., p. xx.

[63] Ibid., p. xxi.

[64] Ibid., p. xxii.

characters" and deviations from the "original forms" giving rise to spurious characters.[65] The existing state of Bengali, as a language, was representative of the natives: lacking a sense of coherence and uniformity. Language and culture were imbued with the characteristics of a nation; the natives were emasculated and deviant, awaiting British colonization, akin to the fact that this scribal culture awaited print culture for progress. The spatial realm of the communications circuit mimicked and replicated the ideologies of the political.[66]

Halhed was operating within existing Western ideologies where the British nation was construed as masculine in contrast to the effeminate colonies. Mrinalini Sinha makes a similar argument in *Colonial Masculinity: The "Manly Englishman" and the "Effeminate Bengali" in the Late Nineteenth Century*, when she states that the social constructs of the manly Englishman and the effeminate Bengali in nineteenth-century India were a result of the emerging dynamics between colonial and nationalist politics and "is best captured in the logic of colonial masculinity."[67] The contours of colonial masculinity were shaped in the context of an "imperial social formation that included both Britain and India."[68] The figures of the "manly

---

[65] Ibid., p. 3.

[66] Vidyasagar was to echo this criticism fifty years later.

[67] Mrinalini Sinha, *Colonial Masculinity: The 'Manly Englishman' and the 'Effeminate Bengali' in the Late Nineteenth Century* (New York: St. Martin's Press, 1995), p. 1.

[68] Ibid., p. 2.

Englishman" and the "effeminate Bengali *babu*," according to Sinha, "were produced by, and helped to shape, the shifts in the political economy of colonialism in the late nineteenth century."[69] Though Sinha analyses nineteenth century colonial Bengal, the ideological contrasts of British masculinity and colonial effeminacy can be traced back to a hundred years ago, as Halhed makes clear.

There is nothing intrinsic to print for the technology to be considered as masculine and rational in comparison to manuscript texts. The characteristics of masculinity were socially ascribed to printed texts. In the early modern period in England, for example, writers were hesitant to see their works being printed, or to be seen ideologically and physically as involved in the marketplace of printers and publication. For the female writer, Jody Greene argues, publication was akin to prostitution, while the male writers shared this anxiety more acutely.[70] The act of publication, that is, submitting one's works to the press, made the writer vulnerable to charges of sexual deviance and indecent exposure. "The male writer," according to Wendy Wall, "always trades on his vulnerability when he agrees to play the female role and be 'pressed' for the public."[71] By the seventeenth century, in England, increased literacy, the

---

[69] Ibid., p. 3.

[70] Jody Greene, "Francis Kirkman's Counterfeit Authority: Autobiography, Subjectivity, Print," *PMLA* 121(1): 17-32.

[71] Wendy Wall, *The Imprint of Gender: Authority and Publication in the English Renaissance* (Ithaca, Cornell UP, 1993), p. 182.

growth of cities and the flow of international capital improved print technology, and authors were more willing to make public works that would have a century ago been limited to private consumption. This caused an explosion in the number of printed books, doing away with how print was conceived. In eighteenth century England, print was seen at the apex of the communication system. For Halhed, writing in 1783, print was imbued with all the characteristics of the British nation and construed as vigorous, rational and truthful.

Scribal-manuscript culture, on the other hand, was defined as archaic and not very reliable. Halhed represents these elements of inauthenticity as inherent in the behavioural habits of the natives, stating that it was with "obstinate and inviolable obscurity the Jentoos conceal … the Mysteries of their faith."[72] This particular grammar text, like other books printed by the scholar-administrators of the East India Company, would undo by making public the concealment, "obscurity" and archaic-ness of scribal knowledge. Halhed was engaged in revealing the knowledge systems that were "shut up in the libraries of Brahmins,"[73] and in undoing the "impenetrable reserve" of the Hindus.[74] While describing the efforts that were taken to write the grammar book, he says that he followed a very clear "set of

---

[72] Halhed, *A Grammar*, p. x.

[73] Ibid., p. iii.

[74] Ibid., p. xi.

rules" and in as "comprehensive" a manner as he could "devise" but the "task was rendered very laborious by the great multiplicity of observations" that he had collected.[75] For Halhed, modern print capitalism would give "a new fixity to language" allowing for a sense of "antiquity" of language" central to the formation of a modern consciousness.[76] Therefore, the realm of print culture mimics the ideological realm of the political, making colonial rule possible.

Establishing print and a public culture in India

When the English came to India, they carried certain notions of how print was to be, and how it was to operate, despite the fact that the socio-economic conditions that had given rise to such a notion of print in England were absent in India. Newspapers and journals were printed in India, but they addressed a very specific readership, and they were comprehensible mostly to readers who were intellectually and socially connected to England. Though newspapers were being printed around the 1780s in India, it does seem strange that within three decades, there could be immense validation of print, a glorification of its rational and argumentative characteristics. In the *Calcutta Journal,* in 1819, the editorial states:

---

[75] Ibid., pp. xviii-xix.

[76] Benedict Anderson. *Imagined Communities. Imagined Communities: Reflections on the Origin and Spread of Nationalism* (New York: Verso, 1991), p. 44.

We have indeed been accused … of giving
too free utterance to sentiments which it has
not been the custom to disseminate through
the medium of the Indian press. In India, we
have no hesitation in saying that the different
Journals published in the country, are, for
more than half the British population who are
immured in the interior of the country and to
whom new books are most inaccessible, the
only medium through which they can keep up
the knowledge either of literary productions,
or scientific discoveries; and those who do not
read them, must necessarily remain ignorant
of a thousand truths interesting to philosophy
and humanity, as marking the rapid strides
with which the present age is advancing
towards the perfection in both.

England, as we have said before, owes her
superiority to other nations, chiefly to the
freedom of her press, and the wide diffusion
of information, among her people. … in
India, every heart that boasts of being
animated by British feelings must not only
rejoice in this distinction, but feel a veneration
for its causes. … The Newspaper press has
become a more powerful engine by which to
promulgate opinions and govern intellect than
ever before existed; than could have been

anticipated by any former age; or than can be
conceived by foreigners who do not
understand, or by natives who have not
studied its economy.[77]

The small group of white residents were connected to each
other through print, locally and globally, and it was through
print that they established a public space. Narratives that
emerged from within the realm of print, bound the English
residents to form a notion of imperial identity. The
plethora of print culture in the form of newspapers,
journals and books formed a print-induced sub-public
sphere.

---

[77] *Calcutta Journal.* July 1, No.123 (1819): 1-2.

Editorial in the Calcutta Journal.

THE CALCUTTA JOURN

OR,

Political, Commercial, and Literary Gazette.

Vol. IV.]   THURSDAY, JULY 1, 1819.

Published Daily, with the exception of Mondays,—and accompanied with occasional Engravings, illustrative of Antiquities the Arts,—at a Subscription price of Eight Rupees per Month, and Half a Rupee for each Plate issued.

General Summary of News.

In entering upon a Fourth Volume of our labours, we look back with pleasure on the success that has attended them; and we rejoice that the free and unshackled expression of public opinion, and the firm adherence to the cause of public right, have met that reward in the approbation of British bosoms, which it must be the pride of every Englishman to see bestowed on those doctrines and principles to which his country owes her pre-eminence over every other nation on the face of the globe.

We have indeed been accused, (and we feel no reproach in adding justly,) of giving too free utterance to sentiments which it has not been the custom to disseminate through the medium of the Indian Press. We may have over-stepped the limits of judicious restrictions, we may have offended public dignity, and wounded private feeling. But as it is undeniably true that all men do not *feel* with equal warmth, so is it indisputable that the pen of one writer, hitherto unrestrained by any consideration but that of truth, may *express* such feelings as direct it, with less of ambiguity and ——, caution, than the pens of others more trained and disciplined to the task.

Who is there, however, among our accusers will dare deny the omnipotence of public opinion, when frankly and unequivocally expressed? and who is there that does not regard the public Journals of the day as the fit and proper organs of its expression?

As society can neither be formed originally, nor afterwards kept together, except by the use of words, every abuse of this distinctive human faculty, must tend necessarily to the corruption of all social ties. Consequently all who are entrusted with the power of committing words to writing, are traitors to their duty whenever they neglect by their public labours to excite the generous passions, to demonstrate useful truths, to add charms to virtue, and to direct the public opinion to the promotion of national prosperity.

Men of letters, says an elegant Italian writer, are independent mediators between the Government,—which applies to force alone and has a natural tendency to despotism,—and the People, who have no less natural inclination towards licentiousness and slavery.

The proof of these principles is in the history of all nations; and the more we exult in the utility of Literature, the more we should declaim against the vanity and the baseness both of those who sell their abilities to tyrants, and of those who employ them in administering to the odious passions and the capricious follies of the multitude.

The free and philosophic spirit of our nation, exclaims a Briton, has been the theme of admiration to the world. This is the proud distinction of Englishmen, and the luminous source of all their glory. Shall we then forget the magnified sentiments of our ancestors, to prate in the the mother or the nurse about our good old pr is not the way to defend the cause of Truth. It that our fathers maintained it, in the brilliant peri tery. Prejudice may be trusted to guard the o short space of time, while Reason slumbers in the if threatter sink into a lethargy, the former will standard for herself.

The sentiment expressed by the author of t Questions, is one which should be ever present t and deserves to be written in letters of gold. W our motto, and shall be proud to serve under a ba with so noble a sentiment, and unfolding so u truth.

" Philosophy, Wisdom, and Liberty, support He who will not reason, is a bigot;—he who cann and he who dares not, is a slave."

There are not wanting, indeed, those who a periodical Journals which appear rapidly, while d highly, the publication of which is slower and at intervals; notwithstanding it frequently happens tents of the latter are chiefly made up from the d of information which have appeared from time to former. Some of the greatest ornaments of Li ever, from Steele and Addison, down to Johnso were occupied in thus directing the taste and t the public, and the great Leviathan of Englis he has been called, very highly eulogizes this agreeable way of disseminating important and u

In India, we have no hesitation in saying th Journals published in the country, are, for more British population who are immured in the country and to whom new books are almost in only medium through which they can keep ledge either of political events, literary producti tific discoveries; and those who do not read the sarily remain ignorant of a thousand truths inter losophy and humanity, as marking the rapid stri the present age is advancing towards perfection

England, as we have said before, owes her other nations, chiefly to the freedom of her pre diffusion of information among her people; and profound maxim that " Knowledge is Strength" rified than in the enviable distinction which a India, every heart that boasts of being anim feelings must not only rejoice in this distinction, neration for its cause; and inclination as well as should conceive, prompt them to the encourage tant possessions of that which has first given maintained them to the mother country; namely,

THE PUBLIC SPHERE IN CALCUTTA. 1780-

Print emerged in Bengal under colonial rule, and this historical event determines how we theorize about the evolution of a print-induced eighteenth century imperial public sphere. I refer to this public sphere as "imperial" as it was specific to the English reading audience, who used print to communicate within themselves in India and across continents, for both social and professional reasons. The print culture that developed, though circumscribed within a small English community as has been described in the preceding sections, was highly sophisticated. This colonial, imperial public sphere is distinct from the European concept of the public sphere, which came into being in the eighteenth century in England as a result of the gradual breakdown of the feudal structure and operated, as Júrgen Habermas argues, separate from the state and civil society, allowing "private people [to] come together as a public"—

in order to engage in criticism of the State, and in the process, promoting democratic participation.[78] A central premise in this Habermasian theory was that the identities of the participants were irrelevant as a group of individuals were willing to come together in order to exchange in critical debate. This very act of doing away with the particularities of the individuals is an impossible endeavor, specifically in the colonial context as we cannot homogenize the Indian reading public.[79]

Despite the fact that the realm of early print culture only catered to the needs of the English residents, it would be too simplistic to blow away this as being too minor an episode in terms of cultural transformation. We do have to keep in mind that firstly, this realm was going to subsequently hegemonize Indian society, and as a

---

[78] Jurgen Habermas, *The Structural Transformation of the Public Sphere*, trans. Thomas Burger (Cambridge: MIT Press, 1989), p. 27.

[79] Not surprisingly, such a position, however emancipatory in theory, has received a lot of negative critical attention. (After all, the print reading public in India in the last two decades of the eighteenth century could not have been but those who knew how to read English!) *The Black Public Sphere* (ed. The Black Public Sphere Collective, Chicago: University of Chicago Press, 1995) argues for the impossibility of conceptualizing the emergence and presence of African American public spaces within the Habermas-ian model, and instead re-articulates the very premises of what constitutes the black public sphere. Feminist critiques target the Habermas-ian notion of the "internally coherent, homogeneous civil public space" as it attains its unity by "banishing its own particularity" and instead, what is proposed is the presence of "multiple" public spheres. Nancy Fraser's post-bourgeois notions of the public sphere state that civil society was constructed through the exclusion of women, and instead she theorizes on the possibility of multiple public spaces co-existing; *Unruly Practices: Power, Discourse, and Gender in Contemporary Social Theory* (Minneapolis: University of Minnesota Press, 1989) and *Justice Interruptus* (New York: Routledge, 1997); as does Michael Warner in *Publics/Counterpublics* (Cambridge: Zone Books, 2003).

consequence, would serve as a prototype for all future printing ventures. This particular form of cultural engagement is best seen as an example of cultural hegemony, where a politically subordinate group emulates and replicates something from a dominant group, and in this case it would be the manner in which the natives learnt about print culture. In the *Prison Notebooks*, Antonio Gramsci poses the issue of how and why subordinate groups seem to consent to their own domination; in other words, when and under what circumstances do people consent to be ruled by a dominant group (or a set of institutions).[80] The realm of culture was one means (rather than simply economic or military) whereby control of the dominant group was gained by the "seemingly spontaneous consent given by the great masses of the population to the general direction imposed on social life by the dominant fundamental group."[81] Cultural hegemony is a relationship between the powerful and the less powerful groups in society. There were many aspects of British culture and technology that were imitated by the subordinate groups and willingly so. Within a few years, there were numerous newspapers being published by the Britishers, and the natives would soon learn about print culture and replicate this realm of letters.

---

[80] Antonio Gramsci, *Selections from the Prison Notebooks*. Translated and edited by Quintin Hoare and Geoffrey Nowell Smith. (New York: International Publishers, 1971), p.12.

[81] Ibid., p. 12.

In the last two decades of the eighteenth century, with the publication of numerous newspapers and books, a sub public republic of letters was formed that was inflected with notions of diaspora and imperialism. Empire of different kinds was in the minds of the English people across the globe. P.J. Marshall writes that the death of the American empire and the birth of the new Indian one occurred at the same time period between 1750 and 1783.[82] He writes that in 1765, the "British EIC was allowed the grant of the Bengal diwani- which was to be the basis of the new empire; in the same year, the weakness of American rule in North America was made evident in the resistance to the Stamp Act" and fifteen years or so later, "Britain was engaged in a war in north America against the local population, supported by the French" while in India, the "EIC and royal forces were fighting against a formidable coalition of Indian powers, also supported by French intervention."[83] Such discourses of empire were dominant both within England and in the colonies. The movement of print and the numerous acts of reading in the colonies influenced how the Britishers viewed themselves as diasporic imperial citizens. Undoubtedly, in India, they were aided in this process by the East India Company, which allowed newspapers to be distributed that did not need postage.

---

[82] P.J. Marshall, *The Making and Unmaking of Empires. Britain, India and America c. 1750-1783* (New York: Oxford University Press, 2005).

[83] Ibid., pp. 1-2.

Print and the emergence of a white city in Calcutta

Print, like many other aspects of eighteenth century Western society, was carried across to Calcutta. When discussing the nature and need of these transferences, it is necessary to understand the relevance and importance of print in the everyday lives of the British community that lived in Calcutta in the last two decades of the eighteenth century. The city became a repository of many things that were British, and was able to attract a wide array of people from every spectrum of society, rich and poor. Many who came were younger sons with no taste for the ministry and little prospect in England. India was a dumping ground for surplus males of the upper and middle classes who then had to make their fortunes as a matter of survival. If the elder son died they would be recalled to inherit, otherwise it was understood that they had to make their own way. The East, with its tales of easily obtainable unfathomable wealth, was the destination for many from the influential and rich families of England. A city was therefore built that catered to this large civilian population and the latter half of the eighteenth century saw the emergence of a miniature, Westernised city in Calcutta, with all the accoutrements and trappings of Western social habits, unlike the first Calcutta, before it was destroyed by Sirajuddaulah in 1756, which was a much more 'Eastern' city of palaces. Early British 'nabobs' were also much more Indianised than sahibs were later to be. Calcutta was rebuilt in a more Western mode by Clive, in keeping with the socio-civic changes that were taking place in eighteenth century British towns; for example, a recent study of British towns in the middle of the century has revealed that there was an "explosion in the demand for and provision of high status leisure."[84] Facilities for enjoyment, like those that existed in an English county town or in a popular resort came into existence in increasing profusion in the white town of Calcutta.[85]

At the end of the eighteenth century, the white population in Calcutta was quite small. In fact, part of the population was a migrant one and sailors comprised a large number. Often they stayed behind and joined the work force as there were ample job opportunities for poor white men. By the mid eighteenth century, there were European domestic servants, artisans and shopkeepers.[86] Builders, tailors, coachmakers, watchmakers, carvers set up their businesses employing Indian craftsmen; dancing and music teachers held classes for members of the rich community and Calcutta was known as a "settlement dominated by wealthy men who lived high."[87]

The white elite of Calcutta prided themselves

---

[84] Peter Borsay, *The English Urban Renaissance: Culture and Society in the Provincial Town, 1660-1770* (Oxford: Oxford University Press, 1989), p. 117.

[85] P.J. Marshall. "The White Town of Calcutta under the Rule of the East India Company," *Modern Asian Studies* 34.2 (May): 307-331, 324.

[86] Ibid., pp. 309-310.

[87] Ibid., p. 312.

on having created in India an environment in which the best of contemporary British institutions were faithfully reproduced. … White Calcutta under the Company was a remarkably British place. … Its development was largely unplanned and its main services, such as drainage, roads and police, were of a low standard. But it had individual buildings of considerable ambition … and its wealthy citizens enjoyed many amenities: books, theatre, music and learned societies.[88]

The city developed in a haphazard manner. The municipal services of the city which were provided by the Company were not in good shape. European architects designed houses that were built in grand, classical styles and not suited for the climate.[89] Churches, schools and orphanages were also built. The prospects of making a fortune were very bright. Banking and trading houses were set up.[90] Apart from those who were directly employed by the East India Company, there grew a class of rich white elites who were involved in different capacities with the numerous civic institutions that cropped up: "partners in the private banks, insurance companies and the ubiquitous agency houses, … which managed shipping, indigo factories and a

---

[88] Ibid., p. 328.

[89] Ibid., p. 316.

[90] Ibid., pp. 310-318.

wide range of [trading] activities."[91] By 1769, the East India Company had started to implement British laws. With the establishment of the Supreme Court in 1774 that dealt with litigation involving both the Europeans and Indians, lawyers were able to reap enormous profits.

By the end of the eighteenth century, many socio-institutional and commercial changes had taken place in Calcutta. The warp and woof of the social existence of the city was dependent on print and its absence was considered an impediment in carrying out their day-to-day socio-civic businesses. Print was needed in order to conduct legal transactions; shopkeepers and traders needed to print advertisements and catalogues in order to sell their goods. Moreover, the British administration needed printed forms and stationery to document its work. Most of the printed material comprised non-literary texts. In order for the printing trade to sustain itself, the presses were involved in the mundane job of printing stationery, handbills, advertisements, catalogues, legal and mercantile blank forms, calendars and almanacs, registers and lists of the employees of the Company and of the European residents of Calcutta. The English community engaged with all the mundane aspects of their everyday lives through print. Thomas Watley, a printer, advertised what would be typically sold from a printer's shop: "Blank bonds, powers of attorney, letters of attorney, respondentia bonds, bills of lading, bills of exchange, printed wills, large and small,

---

[91] Ibid., p. 313.

policies of insurance, with and without the arbitration clause, and of all descriptions, assignments for the disposal of Officers' privileges, handsome ruled paper for music."[92] Such advertisements would have targeted the residents of the white town.[93]

Newspapers comprised a significant bulk of the locally printed material and catered to the small English population in Calcutta. In *Printing in Calcutta to 1800*, Graham Shaw documents the number of presses that were in operation till 1800; from 1780 to 1790, there were between 3 and 5 presses continually in operation, and from 1791 to 1799, between seven and ten active in each year. The presses were mostly concerned with the printing of newspapers, and the increase reflects the opening of newspaper offices in Calcutta in 1791-2. The printing press of the East India Company, the Honourable Company's Press, was the most prolific printing press in Calcutta before 1800. Out of the forty printers, before 1800, only six were not associated with the printing of newspapers; "Lotteries crowd on lotteries, and newspapers on newspapers, but the projectors do not seem to consider where the money to support them is to come from."[94] Statistics reveal that in the last twenty years of the

---

[92] *Calcutta Gazette*, October 18, 1792, XVIII.

[93] Pre-1800, all these socio-civic and legal forms of communication and transaction would have been undertaken through handwritten texts. Is it possible, therefore, to argue that when printed, mechanically reproduced texts replaced handwritten texts, an epistemic shift took place.

[94] *Calcutta Chronicle*. Jan 1, 1793, 7, 363, 2.

eighteenth century in Calcutta, twenty four weekly newspapers and monthly magazines were published.

Why were there, though, so many newspapers? More newspapers meant more advertisements as a large section of the newspapers was filled with them and they were an important source of income for the owners. Many servants of the Company invested in presses and in printing ventures, hoping for fast returns. One investor, Mr. Stocqueler, wrote that he sold his newspaper, *The Englishman,* in 1842 for 13,000 pounds, having purchased it for 1,800 pounds eight years previously.[95] Huge profits were possible because of the high rate of subscription and the income that was generated from advertisements. But, more often than not, newspaper ventures failed. Apart from this economic reason of profit, we also have to take into account the fact that this illogical equation between the number of readers and the available kinds of print can partially be explained if we consider the nature of print culture in eighteenth century Calcutta. Certain characteristics of print culture that we find in Calcutta are also evident in the nature of print in Georgian England. The disproportionate spurt of the growth of newspapers in Calcutta is emblematic of the commercialization of print culture in Georgian England, where by 1695, with the lapse of the Licensing Acts in England—meaning that that the government could not monitor publications—printing

---

[95] Mrinal Kanti Chanda, *The History of the English Press in Bengal* (Calcutta: K.P. Bagchi, 1988), pp. 394-397.

presses grew in an unprecedented manner. Some of the fundamental ideas surrounding the realm of print culture in Georgian England spilled onto the metropole of Calcutta.

BOOK ADVERTISING AND PRINT

No eighteenth-century book in England emerged from the printer without "pages of advertisements, printed or pasted onto the back," thus allowing for print to promote print.[96] Consumer fetishism was not limited to the use of material things, and a similar desire is evident in how printed texts were published and consumed in Calcutta. The advertisements in the newspapers allow us to gauge the nature of the communication network between author, reader, printer, and publisher that was evident in Calcutta. The newspapers and books that were printed in Calcutta, based on subscription readership, ensured the printers a sense of economic viability. This model of subscription publication was a system in use in eighteenth century England. Till the seventeenth century, there had been

---

[96] Barbara Benedict, p. 7.

censorship in England, allowing the government control and surveillance of the kinds of books that were printed, and the number of books that could be printed. With the lapse of the Licensing Act in 1695, a free sphere of print culture evolved, without systematic government intervention. John Brewer describes the emergence of this realm of eighteenth century printers and publishers.[97] In 1689, the world of printing was limited to a few sections of London in St. Paul's Churchyard and Paternoster Row, dominated by a powerful trade guild, and was a community where everyone knew everybody else. But a hundred years later, the publishing industry had grown and in 1785, John Pendred wrote the first guide to English publishing which covered the provinces: *The London and Country Printers, Booksellers and Stationers Vade Mecum.* What "had begun as a London trade had become a national business."[98] The rise of the periodical press made it possible for the professional writer to emerge, and have a career based solely on writing. Commercial publishing meant the bookseller had the upper hand in determining what kinds of books were to be printed, displayed, and were sales-worthy. Subscription made it possible for the inevitable commercial viability in the market place, and the independence of the author as it implied a certain amount of sales, which covered production and distribution costs. The eighteenth century

---

[97] John Brewer, "Authors, Publishers and the Making of Literary Culture," in *The Book History Reader,* ed. David Finkelstein and Alistair McCleery (London and New York: Routledge, 2002).

[98] Ibid., p. 244.

saw subscription publication emerge, bringing together the interests of the author, patron and bookseller. The subscriber had become the patron—which in the earlier centuries was the role played by the Court or wealthy individuals. This model was followed by the printers and writers in Calcutta, and ensured some degree of economic independence for emergent writers.

With the emergence of subscription readership the relationship between the author, reader and printer changed. Newspapers played a role in disseminating news about new publishing ventures, becoming a medium though which new printing enterprises were advertised and therefore, it was through print that a desire for more print was created and sustained. For example, an advertisement for a new weekly publication, the *Chittagong Herald,* was announced in the following manner in the *Calcutta Chronicle* (fig. 16): "Three gentlemen have stepped forward in support of this agreeable 'Publication' and look forward to entertain their 'small settlement' every Sunday." A poem was enclosed, addressed to the Public: "Ye gentlemen and ladies all, / Who live at Chittagong, / On you the Herald means to call / Each Sunday, with a song;" and the poem ends with a few lines from the printer, "Great-Sir, I beg you'll tell the town, / My types are very few; / My press is old and broken down, / With scarce a single screw."[99] By informing the readers of new literary and journalistic ventures, and also by often making requests for monetary

[99] *Calcutta Chronicle*, March 13 (1792): 4.

advances, a subscription-based readership was formed.

It is fascinating to examine the nature of the books that were printed and sold by the printers in Calcutta; advertisements reveal the specific nature of what was being printed.[100] *History of the Bible and Catechetical Instruction with a Persian Translation, Sold for the Benefit of the Protestant Mission in Bengal.* Grammar books were written in volumes: "Gilchrist's *Grammar*, Chapter III, is now ready for Delivery, at the Chronicle Office, to such Subscribers who send for it. The Fourth Chapter will be published shortly, due Notice will be given." The printers served as book sellers, and there was an absence of a separate establishment for books to be published. There were advertisements for books that were to be published, and waited for buyers; "Speedily will be published an edition of *Angelo's School of Fencing, with a General Explanation of the Principal Attitudes and Positions Peculiar to the Art.* [it is only on request] – Those gentlemen who are inclined to favor the publication will be pleased to signify their intentions to Mr. Upjohn." Often, these proposals would be in addition to lengthy descriptions of the text that was to be printed (fig.18):[101] "Proposals for Publishing by Subscription, *The Musical Olio, or Chearful Companion: Being A Collection of Songs, sung at The Anacreontick Society, The Beef-Steak Club, and Several Other Convivial Meetings;* by Dibdin and Others. The Work to be printed on English Foolscap, with a beautiful Type; to

---

[100] *Calcutta Chronicle*, April 3 (1792): 3.

[101] *Calcutta Chronicle*, Nov. 6 (1792).

Advertisements for a new publication.

POETS' CORNER.

TO THE EDITOR OF THE CHRONICLE.

SIR,

A new Publication made its appearance here on Sunday last, call'd THE CHITTAGONG HERALD; as your News-paper Gentry in Calcutta. I enclose you the Editor's Address to the Public, and request you will indulge me by giving it a place in your neat Chronicle, for its more general circulation. The peculiar neatness of the print—uniform and correct to a degree—the facetious figure on the top, and judicious mode of placing him, with the words, " I know F——" underneath, exceeds all description. I am credibly informed that three Gentlemen have dropped forward in supp. t of this agreeable Publication; and as their declared purpose is to furnish entertainment through our small settlement, on every Sunday, I have not a doubt of their pleasing endeavours being covered with success.

I am, Yours,
NONDESCRIPT.

Chittagong, 18th February, 1792.

Address to the Public.

YE gentlemen and ladies all,
Who live at Chittagong,
On you the Herald means to call
Each Sunday, with a song;

And as he'll e'en do what he can
To make his readers laugh,
He hopes ill-nature ne'er will scan
A single paragraph.

From hill to hill he means to range,
And give you all the news—
Remove the cause at full and change
Whene'er you've got the blues.

From Shawakroofe in Chittagong,
Like Louis Patten's lamp;
Or, as he hangs on air-balloon,
Perhaps to Tippoo's camp.

In gall his pen he ne'er will dip,
His heart's from flander free;
The ladies here no scandal sip,
With Hysson or Bohea.

He, therefore, hopes that all who can,
Will lend their gen'rous aid,
To forward this his weekly plan,
Man, widow, wife, or maid.

For what the men may choose to send,
His thanks shall be the fee;
But when the ladies kindly bend,
A kiss or low congee.

Yet here, perhaps, they'd wish to know,
(The author is so civil)

Advertisements of printed books.

Advertisements of books that were to be printed.

consist of One Hundred and Fifty Pages, and to contain near Two Hundred Songs,—When Fifty copies are subscribed for, the Work will be put to Press. And it is the Compiler's Intention to Print off no more than are really subscribed for. Gentlemen wishing to become Subscribers to the above Work will be pleased to make known their intentions to Mr. A. B. Bone, at the Circulating Library." Vocabulary books were printed:[102] "In the press, and speedily will be published, an extensive Vocabulary, Bengalese and English, Very Useful to teach the natives English, and to assist Beginners in learning the Bengal language. Those who wish for the work, are requested to send their orders to Mr. Upjohn." Books in translation were also printed: "The Following Books, translated from the Persian. May be had on application to Mr. Upjohn at the Printing Office: *Narrative of Transactions in Bengal, Memoirs of Abdulkurreem, Pundnameh – Persian and English, Epitome of Mohammaden Law and The Compendium of Revenue Accounting.*" It is not surprising that printing offices served as booksellers: "for sale, at the printing office, *The Happy Prescription, Comedy in Rhyme. The Two Connoisseurs,*" and another advertisement said, "*New Publication. Lately Published. Dissertation concerning the Landed Property of Bengal.*" There were also bilingual publications: "*The Tootinameh,* now in the press, is a collection of Persian Tales, written expressly for the improvement of young students; and the English part is by a gentleman whose publications have been well received, both here and in Europe, to render into

[102] *Calcutta Chronicle,* April 3 (1792): 3.

English such subjects as the present, with any degree of success is no pleasant or easy task on account of accommodating the sense to a different idiom so as to preserve the spirit of the original and at the same time avoid the ridiculous extremes of stupidity or bombast."[103] The reading public knew about books that were printed from manuscripts: an advertisement stated "Lately published, a correct and elegant edition of *The Works of Hafez*, from a most accurate and valuable copy."[104] Thus, the realm of printed texts—of grammar books, translations, poems—that emerged in the last two decades of the eighteenth century in Calcutta catered to the needs of the Britishers.

Advertisements of vocabulary and grammar books.

[104] *Calcutta Chronicle*, April 3 (1792): 3.

Figure 20: Advertisement of a bilingual translation.

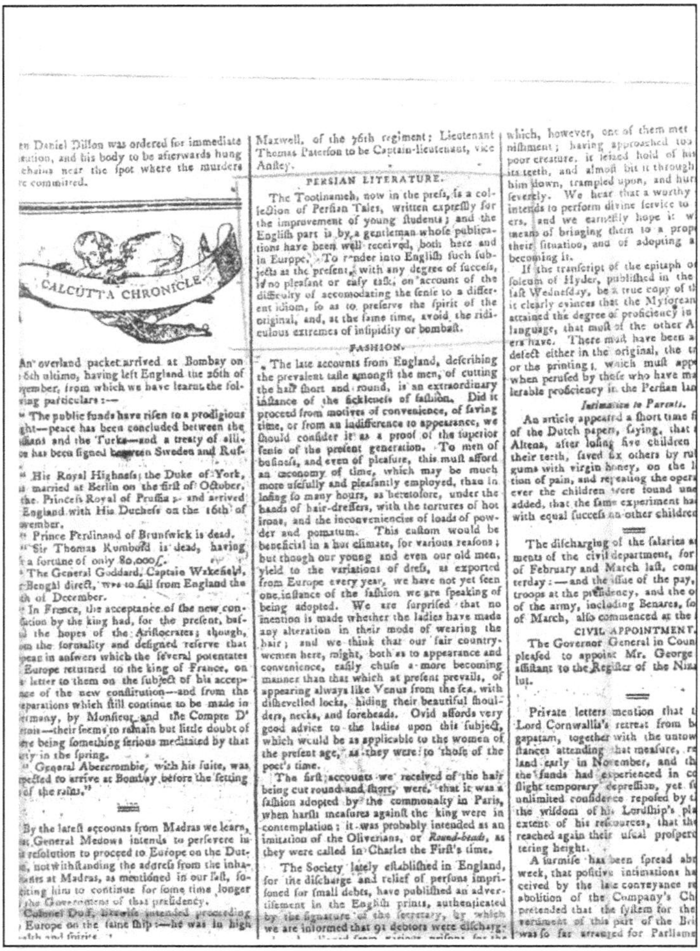

en Daniel Dillon was ordered for immediate cution, and his body to be afterwards hung chains near the spot where the murders re committed.

An overland packet arrived at Bombay on 6th ultimo, having left England the 26th of vember, from which we have learnt the following particulars:—

"The public funds have risen to a prodigious ght—peace has been concluded between the ssians and the Turks—and a treaty of alliance has been signed between Sweden and Russia.

"His Royal Highness, the Duke of York, as married at Berlin on the first of October, the Princess Royal of Prussia ;— and arrived England with His Duchess on the 16th of vember.

"Prince Ferdinand of Brunswick is dead.

"Sir Thomas Rumbold is dead, having t a fortune of only 80,000£.

"The General Goddard, Captain Wakefield, Bengal direct, was to sail from England the th of December.

"In France, the acceptance of the new constitution by the king had, for the present, baffled the hopes of the Aristocrates; though, om the formality and designed reserve that pear in answers which the several potentates Europe returned to the king of France, on letter to them on the subject of his acceptance of the new constitution—and from the eparations which still continue to be made in ermany, by Monsieur and the Compte D'rtois—their seems to remain but little doubt of ere being something serious meditated by that rty in the spring.

"General Abercrombie, with his suite, was pected to arrive at Bombay before the setting of the rains."

By the latest accounts from Madras we learn, at General Medows intends to persevere in s resolution to proceed to Europe on the Dutch, notwithstanding the address from the inhabitants at Madras, as mentioned in our last, soliciting him to continue for some time longer the Government of that presidency.

Colonel Duff, likewise intended proceeding Europe on the same ship:—he was in high

Maxwell, of the 76th regiment; Lieutenant Thomas Paterson to be Captain-lieutenant, vice Anstey.

PERSIAN LITERATURE.

The Tootinameh, now in the press, is a collection of Persian Tales, written expressly for the improvement of young students; and the English part is by a gentleman whose publications have been well received, both here and in Europe. To render into English such subjects as the present, with any degree of success, is no pleasant or easy task, on account of the difficulty of accomodating the sense to a different idiom, so as to preserve the spirit of the original, and, at the same time, avoid the ridiculous extremes of insipidity or bombast.

FASHION.

The late accounts from England, describing the prevalent taste amongst the men, of cutting the hair short and round, is an extraordinary instance of the fickleness of fashion. Did it proceed from motives of convenience, of saving time, or from an indifference to appearance, we should consider it as a proof of the superior sense of the present generation. To men of business, and even of pleasure, this must afford an œconomy of time, which may be much more usefully and pleasantly employed, than in losing so many hours, as heretofore, under the hands of hair-dressers, with the tortures of hot irons, and the inconveniencies of loads of powder and pomatum. This custom would be beneficial in a hot climate, for various reasons; but though our young and even our old men, yield to the variations of dress, as exported from Europe every year, we have not yet seen one instance of the fashion we are speaking of being adopted. We are surprised that no mention is made whether the ladies have made any alteration in their mode of wearing the hair; and we think that our fair country-women here, might, both as to appearance and convenience, easily chuse a more becoming manner than that which at present prevails, of appearing always like Venus from the sea, with dishevelled locks, hiding their beautiful shoulders, necks, and foreheads. Ovid affords very good advice to the ladies upon this subject, which would be as applicable to the women of the present age, as they were to those of the poet's time.

The first accounts we received of the hair being cut round and short, were, that it was a fashion adopted by the commonalty in Paris, when harsh measures against the king were in contemplation: it was probably intended as an imitation of the Oliverians, or *Round-heads*, as they were called in Charles the First's time.

The Society lately established in England, for the discharge and relief of persons imprisoned for small debts, have published an advertisement in the English prints, authenticated by the signature of the secretary, by which we are informed that 91 debtors were discharg-

which, however, one of them met
nishment; having approached too
poor creature, it seized hold of his
its teeth, and almost bit it through
him down, trampled upon, and hur
severely. We hear that a worthy
intends to perform divine service to
ers, and we earnestly hope it w
means of bringing them to a prop
their situation, and of adopting a
becoming it.

If the transcript of the epitaph o
soleum of Hyder, published in the
last Wednesday, be a true copy of th
it clearly evinces that the Mysorean
attained the degree of proficiency in
language, that most of the other A
ers have. There must have been a
defect either in the original, the tr
or the printing, which must app
when perused by those who have ma
lerable proficiency in the Persian lan

Intimation to Parents.

An article appeared a short time f
of the Dutch papers, saying, that
Altena, after losing five children
their teeth, saved six others by ru
gums with virgin honey, on the l
tion of pain, and repeating the opera
ever the children were found una
added, that the same experiment ha
with equal success on other childre

The discharging of the salaries a
ments of the civil department, for
of February and March last, com
terday:—and the issue of the pay,
troops at the presidency, and the o
of the army, including Benares, fo
of March, also commenced at the

CIVIL APPOINTMENT.

The Governor General in Coun
pleased to appoint Mr. George
assistant to the Register of the Niz
lut.

Private letters mention that t
Lord Cornwallis's retreat from b
gapatam, together with the untow
stances attending that measure, r
land early in November, and th
the funds had experienced in c
slight temporary depression, yet s
unlimited confidence reposed by t
the wisdom of his Lordship's pl
extent of his resources, that th
reached again their usual prosper
tering height.

A surmise has been spread ab
week, that positive intimations ha
ceived by the late conveyance r
abolition of the Company's Ch
pretended that the system for the
vernment of this part of the Bri
was so far arranged for Parliame

Conclusion

There was no formal exchange of technology between the natives and the British. One can assume that close interaction with the British made it possible for the natives to emulate the habits of those in power. The native elite of Calcutta were willing to explore and adapt to the new things from the west and their desires were "much stronger than the willingness of Europeans to receive anything in return."[105] By a "mechanism which remains unexplained," architectural styles were imitated by the black town. P. J. Marshall writes that the Indian intelligentsia responded to the European civilization it encountered in a productive fashion. In fact, he argues that "private self indulgence by individual Europeans made a greater contribution to Indian awareness of the west than public policy."[106] The whites established a lavish, British lifestyle for themselves, leaving "abundant pickings for Indians who were minded to take advantage of their prodigality"; cultural habits were diffused in an accidental fashion. This fact is important to keep in mind as it partially explains how print culture was transferred into Calcutta. A high level of sophistication marked the nature of print within the white city of Calcutta, and the natives engaged with this notion of print culture. When we trace the beginnings of print culture in Calcutta, we have to go back to how print developed and was used by the whites who lived in Calcutta at the end of

---

[105] Marshall, "White Town," p. 330.

[106] Ibid., pp. 329, 308.

the eighteenth century.

Moreover, the press initiated a shift in the very nature of how texts were to be written, preserved and disseminated. It initiated a shift in the very method of writing, a shift that involved cultural habits —Indians would sit on the floor and write, unlike Europeans who used tables. Nathaniel Halhed describes it in the following manner: "As they have neither chairs nor tables, their posture in writing is very different from ours: they sit upon their heels, or sometimes upon their hams, while their left hand hold open serves as a desk whereon to lay the paper on which they write, which is kept in its place by the thumb: so that they never write on a large sheet of paper without folding it down to a very small surface."[107] Can we possibly argue that such a shift, which undoes the existing socio-cultural structure, implies a sense of power embodied in the printing press? A similar shift occurred in Europe, in the modern period, with the introduction of printing presses where diverse occupational groups worked with each other in the new workshops that were set up by the early printers. Elisabeth Eisenstein describes the numerous processes that were involved:

> The preparation of copy and illustrative material for printed editions led to a rearrangement of all book-making arts and routines. Not only did new skills, such as

[107] Nathaniel Brassey Halhed, *A Grammar of the Bengal Language*, p. 2.

typefounding and presswork, involve veritable occupational mutations; but the production of printed books also gathered together in one place more traditional variegated skills. In the age of scribes, book-making had occurred under the diverse auspices represented by stationers and lay copyists in university towns; … The advent of printing led to the creation of a new kind of shop structure; to a regrouping which entailed closer contacts among diversely skilled workers and encouraged new forms of cross-cultural interchange. …

Thus it is not uncommon to find former priests among early printers or former abbots serving as editors or correctors. University professors also often served in similar capacities and thus came into closer contact with metal workers and mechanics.[108]

When the printing presses were introduced in Bengal, the hierarchical status between the English and the Indians was maintained. The editors and the master printers were Europeans, many of whom were employed from England, while the compositors were Indians. We learn about the

---

[108] Elizabeth Eisenstein, "Defining the Initial Shift: Some Features of Print Culture" in *The Book History Reader,* ed. David Finkelstein and Alistair McCleery (London and New York: Routledge, 2002), pp. 156-157.

operation of printing presses by narratives that were written:

> The Editor … on reaching his office …
> delivers to him (the head printer) such
> manuscripts, or extracts from other papers
> and periodicals, as are to constitute the
> contents of the journal for the day following.
> The printer then distributes this matter or
> copy … to the compositors … and the galley
> proof … is then delivered to … a reader, to
> examine and correct … superintended by the
> head printer. The galley proofs … are
> collected together late in the evening, when
> there appears no probability of more news,
> correspondence, or advertisements reaching
> the office … Editor or his deputy then selects
> such portion of the matter … as it is
> important…. From this, the subordinate
> printer proceeds to … form a page of the
> paper. The pressmen cover the [iron frames]
> with ink by means of balls composed of
> sheep skins… a proof impression of the
> pages is then taken off and … carefully read
> by the head printer and the Editor after which
> the printing of the whole impression
> commences.[109]

---

[109] J.H. Stoccqueler, "The Calcutta Press," in *Calcutta Quarterly Magazine and Review* 3(Oct.1833): 424-425.

The printer would be European, and a big printing establishment would keep around eighty to a hundred compositors.

HETEROGLOSSIC TEXTS: ENGLISH-NATIVE NEWSPAPERS IN COLONIAL CALCUTTA.

Between 1780 and 1800, many newspapers in Calcutta printed news in multiple languages side by side on the same sheet of paper. This was a moment in the history of newspapers in England and in India that had not happened before and was not replicated subsequently. Any reader of these beautiful multilingual sheets of paper would question as to why such newspapers went out of fashion in a few decades after they were printed. Not only had the new technology of print culture entered India with the Britishers but also, this technology, in the process of establishing itself within a colonial situation, underwent changes on how it was conceptualized. Colonization determined the nature of print culture which is why multilingual newspapers emerged in Calcutta and for a few moments in the history of print culture and of newspapers, there were such heteroglossic texts. The sheer new-ness of the visual text was and is mind-boggling in all respects – specially if we see how radical it was conceptually.

Is it possible that such a multilingual text could only happen in south Asia where a multilingual society exists. In some ways, and unwittingly so, the Britishers captured an aspect of Indian society within these printed texts and the sheer spirit of invention marks these newspapers. The possibilities of what could have been if newspapers had continued to be multilingual are not explored for it denotes an epistemic shift, thus answering a question: what happens when a technology that has its origins in a different social space enters a new geographical locale and how does it change? The heteroglossic nature of Indian society was reflected in how these newspapers were formed; moreover, in some ways, the Britishers were attempting to portray and capture Indian society in these newspapers.

Multilingual texts.

Fine Cambric Mulmulls, 4 bales 30 by 4, Containing
    30 by 3 -do.   30 Pieces.

Do. White Bordered Romauls 2 Bales, 16 in each Piece,

Brandy,
Sugar Candy,   Casks,
Tea,   Tubs,
Box,

Govt. Custom House,
Calcutta, the 12th Jan. 1788.

G. H.

بندر وکیل بتاریخ بیست و هشتم روز ماه جنوری سنه ۱۷۸۸ انگریزی در میان کمپنی...

شراب وغیره

چای   مصرکی   پارچه ساده پدیده سلزده   شراب فرنگی

বড় কমিটীর এইখবর সকলকে দেওয়া যাইতেছে ২৬ আলের...

৩০ ৷৪ হাজা
৩০ ৷৫ হাজা
৫ নাদাপাত্যাদি মাল ২ গাঠী ১৬ থেরী   ২৫০ থান
          ৮৫০ থান

ইতি সন ১৭৮৮ সাল ১২ আহের ইংরেজি সন ১১৯৪ সাল যাঘ

For SALE at the CIRCULATING LIBRARY

Some very elegant Bound

QUARTO and OCTAVO BIBLES

Sahib involvement in native print. The need for heteroglossic print.

What remains a fuzzy unexplored area is whether the natives took up print culture easily enough or was there initial resistance at the advent of the new technology? The nature of print that entered south Asia had evolved since its beginnings three hundred years ago in the west. Even a hundred years ago, there was conflicting attitudes in England towards print technology. Manuscript culture was present even after 1710 and the Act of Queen Anne and it was considered a "competitive if not the dominant mode of transmitting and reading 'literary' and 'academic' materials."[110] This act of clinging on to an "outdated" technology of the fading aristocratic world of letter represented an authorial choice. But obviously enough, there were enormous epistemic shifts made as a result of print and Eisenstein writes about its revolutionary impact on how science was conceptualized:

> The advantages of issuing identical images bearing identical labels to scattered observers who could feed back information to publishers enabled astronomers, geographers, botanists, and zoologists to expand data pools far beyond all pervious limits – even those set by the exceptional resources of the long lasting Alexandrian Museum. … The closed world of the ancients was opened; vast expanses of

---

[110] "Social Authorship and the Advent of Print," p. 12.

space (and later of time) previously associated with divine mysteries became subject to human calculation and exploration.[111]

As a result of print, knowledge could spread in faster methods than had been possible previously. In the western world, the shift that took place from a manuscript culture was a gradual but inevitable one, but we do not really such ambiguities in how print culture was perceived by the natives in Calcutta as the sophisticated social characteristics of late eighteenth century print were transferred on to the colony. In Bengal, the Britishers developed native fonts, which were subsequently made use of by the natives. But, did the availability of fonts make it easier for the natives to make the shift from manuscript to print culture? More importantly and is a question we should be asking at the present is whether native usage was impacted by the fact that the Britishers made use of native fonts? In what can but only be described as being ironical, the Britishers printed multilingual texts but these were subsequently used in a different context altogether by the natives. These texts that were initially printed by the Britishers for their own needs, incidentally represented the multilingual nature of Indian society.

The efforts that were taken to obtain and create fonts and types in Indian languages are little known facts. Many of the newspapers would be beautifully illustrated

---

[111] Eisenstein, pp. 256-257.

with Indian languages and a single page would have Urdu, and Bengali side by side. During the time period that I am referring to - between 1780 and 1820 - these newspapers were only read by the Britishers, which means that the Indian languages only had English readers. In 1830, a report in *The Friend of India* said that before this period, "the press had been confined to Europeans, and the only works in the native languages were printed at their expense and circulated gratis."[112] A question that needs to be answered is: why were there elaborate Indian prints in newspapers that would not necessarily be read by all the English readers of the newspapers?

The larger argument that was used to legitimate British colonization was that it was needed to do good for the natives; this explains to a great extent many of the socio-cultural and technological exchanges that took place between the Britishers and the natives. The relationship is best described in the following manner:

> Britain possesses the means of improvement and instruction beyond most nations in Europe. India on the contrary is ignorant and wretched, while a bounteous Providence is pouring forth upon her almost every blessing which can render a country happy. But it is to Britain alone that she can look for instruction and relief. Did other nations posses the

---

[112] "Art. V. - On the effect of the Native Press in India," *The Friend of India*. Quarterly Series (No. 1): 130-154, p. 133.

means of imparting them in the fullest manner, the opportunity is denied them. How could any other nation interfere so as to gain the confidence of India? It is to Britain alone that Providence has committed this pleasing task, and in a more full and ample manner than has ever been done to any nation at any former period.[113]

The reason that was used to justify the need for colonization was that the Indians needed the Britishers for "improvement and instruction" because as a nation, Britain alone could provide them with the required education as the other nations "lacked" the means of imparting them. Moreover, during the early years of British presence, the task of colonization was seen as a "pleasing" one which would enable the Indians to "gain the[ir] confidence." It would be a meaningful enterprise if we allowed ourselves to view print culture as part of the process of "instruction" accompanying empire and colonization. This implies that we have to consider print as functioning against manuscript culture and regard it as it was considered by the Britishers: a vast systemic and civilizational improvement.

During the initial years of colonization, India was seen as a part of Britain.[114] It would be rather simplistic and

---

[113] Ibid., p. 135.

[114] The loss of the thirteen American colonies is said to have brought to an end the first British empire based on the Atlantic Ocean, and occurred at a time period between 1750 and 1783 which also saw the "first waves of Indian conquests made by the EIC." The British EIC was given the grant of the Bengal diwani in 1765 and in fifteen years, Britain was engaged in a war in North America against the local population. (P. J. Marshall, *The Making*

naïve if we were to interpret this phase of colonization of Bengal as operating within absolute binaries of ruler and ruled. It was important to keep the new British citizens in the colonies happy, and learning the languages made that possible through better communication. In a review of Halhed's grammar book in 1783, a similar concern was articulated:

> Our settlements in the East form deservedly one of the greatest objects of national concern. Populous and rich, our chief attention should be fixed on making them happy and secure....
> ...without an easy and general intercourse with the natives, through the medium of language, no system of regulation, which the wisdom of man may frame, can promise any solid, rational, or permanent establishment of authority and power.
> ... we shall confine our observations to strictures on the history and the usefulness of a language of very high antiquity, spoken by millions of industrious Briitsh subjects, and of great importance, in various lights, towards the proper management of the commercial, military, and revenue departments of Bengal.[115]

The review draws attention to certain fundamental

---

and Unmaking of Empires, p. 1)

[115] "A Review of 'A Grammar of the Bengal Language.'" In *The English Review* (1783): 1-2.

assumptions within which empire was established and these make for interesting speculation; the Bengali language was an example of "novelty, as well as of utility" and therefore, it was brought to public attention. What is equally fascinating is that the reviewer normalizes the publication of such a grammar book and even recommends it to the English reader; he writes that the book presented the readers with "elements of a language hitherto disregarded, and almost unknown in Europe."[116] In some way, this act of being able to codify a native language and transfer it to print technology is seen as an act of British cultural superiority: "Another gentleman employs the extraordinary efforts of a singular and persevering genius in the fabrication of types of a very novel and difficult construction: whilst we find a Governor General, (unlike every description of public men in Britain) amidst all the busy scenes of war and state affairs, cultivating the arts of peace."[117] There is little documented evidence as to whether the natives were critical of how print evolved in Calcutta and the British government's attempts to cultivate such a realm could thus be seen as an act of "peace".

It was not only that print technology symbolized the British colonizers desire to promote the arts of peace but there were some necessary practical reasons to why such heteroglossic texts were printed and circulated amongst the white community. Francis Gladwin, wrote in a letter in

[116] Ibid., p. 12.

[117] Ibid., p. 12.

1784 to the Board of Directors of the EIC as to why a newspaper like *The Calcutta gazette, or Oriental Advertiser* was needed; "[to start a gazette] as it might be made Useful to the Junior part of the Company's Servants by the insertion of Extracts from the most approved Persian Authors; in the original Character with English Translations, and thus facilitate their Improvement in that Language, the study of which has been so frequently recommended to them by the Court of Directors."[118] In the preface to the *Asiatik Miscellany*, Gladwin wrote that it would be an enterprising endeavor to print Persian works alongside English translations:

> And though this part of the Work may, at first sight, seem particularly designed for those who study the Persian language, and will undoubtedly be of singular use to them, it is yet by no means on their account alone, that the extracts appear in that form. The translations will, we trust, be always matter of curiosity and entertainment to English readers also, who in seeing them accompanied by their respective originals, will have no reason to be satisfied, that what is presented to them as a specimen of eastern history or composition, is neither spurious nor disguised by borrowed ornament, but is genuine, pure and unadulterated.[119]

---

[118] Quoted in *A History of the Calcutta Press*, Nair, p. 110.

[119] Quoted in Ibid., pp. 116-117.

British superiority was evident in that print could erase the impure and adulterated parts of a manuscript language. The natives must have accepted this assumption for we find scant criticism against the emergence of native types and print.

THEORIES OF UTILITARIANISM: CAN COLONIZATION MAKE THE NATIVES HAPPY?

India, as a colony, was viewed as a precious possession and such a view is articulated quite strongly in a text like *The Annals of the College of Fort William*,[120] which was written in the early nineteenth century and symptomises some of the basic principles underlying empire formation: the empire should be maintained with the "spirit of enterprise and boldness which acquired it" but it should not "be administered as a temporary and precarious acquisition -- as an Empire conquered by prosperous adventure, and extended by fortunate accident, of which the tenure is as uncertain as the original conquest and successive extension were extraordinary"; the colony would be considered "as a

---

[120] *The Annals of the College of Fort William.*

sacred trust, and a permanent succession."[121]
Notwithstanding such a view about the colony, there is still
no direct reason as to why there was a need to invest so
much intellectual resources into India and what determined
the underlying principles behind colonization? But we do
find that there are abstract concepts of goodness and
happiness that recur over and over again in a text like *The
Annals of the College of Fort William*, which nudge us towards
assuming, that at least, during the initial years of empire
building in India, British imperialism did desire to portray
itself as something more than mere brute power. The
assumption that the act of colonization would lead to the
happiness of the natives is clearly an utilitarian one and is
best summarized in John Stuart Mill's definition of
Utilitarianism when he described it as that "creed which
accepts as the foundation of morals, Utility, or the Greatest
Happiness Principle, holds that actions are right in
proportion as they tend to promote happiness, wrong as
they tend to produce the reverse of happiness."[122] In the
"Introduction" to the *Annals*, which mostly puts forward a
rationale of the newly established College of Fort William,
the English readers are told that the "general happiness and
prosperity of the country" depended on the "conduct" of
the civil servants of the EIC, and they would be unable to
engage in communication unless they were conversant with
the "Native languages" and the laws and customs of the

---

[121] Ibid., p. xi.

[122] Stuart Mill, *Utilitarianism* (London: Longmans, Green, Reader and Dyer, 1871), pp. 9-10.

land.[123] It was the "sacred duty, true interest, honour and policy of the British nation" that compelled the British government to rule for the "prosperity and happiness" of the people of India.[124] In a similar manner, it was argued that the English would preserve Indian culture in a more comprehensive fashion than had been, and therefore the need to preserve manuscripts was that it would eventually lead to the happiness of the Indians:

> The preservation and augmentation of the Collection of Eastern Manuscripts, afford the only means of arresting the progressive destruction of Oriental learning. Since the dismemberment of the Muslim, those works have been dispersed over India, and have been exposed to the injuries and hazards of time, accident and neglect. It is worthy of the ambition of this great Empire to employ every effort of its influence in preserving from destruction and decay, these valuable records of Oriental history, Science and Religion.[125]

By engaging with the natives and by teaching them, the Indian subjects would also have a more favourable view of the British rulers. There would diffuse among them "a spirit of civilization and an improved sense of those genuine principles of morality and virtue," that would

---

123 *Annals*, p. iii-iv.

124 Ibid., p. xv.

125 Ibid., p. 114.

promote their happiness and establish a stable British empire.[126]

The civil servants were not the "agents of a commercial concern" but were the "ministers and officers of a Powerful Sovereign."[127] Their education in the College of Fort William would help them to discharge their duties in a manner that would allow them to "honour" the "British name in India" and would lead to the "prosperity and happiness" of the "Native subjects."[128] They would learn to perform the duty of ruling "the extensive and valuable dominions" the nation had acquired in India, for by discharging this duty, depended the "prosperity and permanency" of the Empire.[129] The education of the civil servants would not be exclusively "European or Indian" but would involve the combined principles of Asian and European policy and government." Their education would be of a mixed nature, the "foundation" laid in England and "the superstructure systematically completed in India."[130] The College of Fort William was meant to teach the civil servants so that they could understand the existing laws and regulations, thus "enabling" them to discharge their duty.[131] Good administration would eventually create happy subjects:

---

[126] Ibid., p. 115

[127] Ibid. p. iv.

[128] Ibid., p. v.

[129] Ibid., p.19.

[130] Ibid., p. xii.

[131] Ibid., p. 92.

The due administration of just laws within these flourishing and populous provinces, is not only the foundation of the happiness of millions of people, but the main pillar of the vast fabric of the British Empire in Asia; the mainspring of our Empire is situated here...

... the excellence of the general spirit of these laws is attested by the noblest proof of just, wise, and honest government; by the restoration of happiness, tranquility, and security, to an oppressed and suffering people, and by the revival of agriculture, commerce, manufacture, and general opulence in a declining and impoverished country.[132]

The fundamental premise was that the natives would welcome British presence and would want to be ruled and such an explanation partially explains the enormous flow of culture and technology into India. It is within this Utilitarian interpretative model that we can understand the enormous efforts taken to not only create native fonts, but also the need to set up the institution of print culture in an elaborate manner.

---

[132] Ibid., pp. 93-94.

Involving people and technology: the processes behind the creation of native font.

In a succinct commentary on how it took centuries for print to develop in the west, unlike the rapid manner in how it evolved in Calcutta, Halhed, in *The Grammar of the Bengal Language*, summarizes the efforts taken by Charles Wilkins to perfect the native types:

> With a rapidity unknown in Europe, he surmounted all the obstacles which necessarily clog the first rudiments of a difficult art, as well as the disadvantages of solitary experiment; and has thus singly on the first effort exhibited his work in a state of perfection which in every part of the world has appeared to require the united the united improvements of different projectors, and the gradual polish of successive ages.[133]

When the East India Company government established its printing press, Wilkins was its first head. But as we look closely at the nitty gritty details of the workings of the Srirampur Mission Press, one realizes that natives were active participants in the process of how technology was exchanged; Joshua Marshman, while describing Panchanan's efforts, wrote: "[with his] assistance we created a letter foundry, and although he is dead now, he

---

[133] Halhed, pp. xxiii-xxiv.

had so full communicated his art to a number of others, that they carry forward the work of type casting, and even of cutting the matrices with a degree of accuracy which would not disgrace European artists."[134] Largely due to the efforts of William Carey, there was interaction between the Srirampur Mission press and the College of Fort William and many of the books written by the scholars of the college were printed in this press. Carey appointed many good scribes in different languages. The Bengali letters were engraved on the basis of a sample prepared by Kali Kumar Ray, the Bengali copyist of the College. Kali Kumar Ray must have been a scribe. What is interesting is that both natives and Englishmen were involved in the process of making types, therefore making the evolution of Indian print a collaborative venture.[135]

Panchanan taught the art of cutting types to Manohar, who was to become his son in law. Marshman described Manohar as "an expert and elegant workman who was subsequently employed for forty years at the Srirampur Press and to whose exertions and instructions Bengal is indebted for the various beautiful fonts of the Bengali, Nagree, Persian, Arabic and other characters

---

[134] From Sisir Kumar Das' *Sahibs and munshis: an account of the College of Fort William* (Calcutta: Orion Publications, 1978), p. 96.

[135] *Annals:* "Many learned Natives are now attached to the Institution, who have been invited to Fort William by my special authority from different parts of Asia. … The sudden dismission of the learned Natives attached to the College would therefore be an act of manifest injustice on the grounds already stated; it would also be an act of the most flagrant impolicy; nor would it be consistent either with the interest or the honour of the Company in India, …pp. l-li.

which have been gradually introduced into the different printing establishments."[136] Over a span of around thirty years, between 1801-1830, the Srirampur Mission press printed books in over fifty languages.

A lot of intellectual labor went into the process of making types and perfecting the font. John Gilchrist made some changes to the printing of the Perso-Arabic scripts. In 1802, he wrote to the College Council: "as the types and printing materials which Mr. Gladwin presented to College are probably the best now to be procured, I request you will state to College my wish to take charge of, and employ them for the good of my department here, in the works I am about to publish in Hindoostanee language."[137] He also promised to return the types when needed to the College Council and thus was started the Hindoostane Press. Till then, there were some presses in operation: the Chronicle Press, Stuart and Cooper Press, Ferris and Greenway Press, and the Hurkaru Press. On 20th June, Gilchirst wrote to the College Council that he had made major improvements in 'Oriental typography' on the "European principle of separating words by spaces and joining the letters of each vocable, as much as possible." Lumsden subsequently made changes to Gilchrist's innovations. In 1805, he presented plans of improving the existing types in Persian and for establishing a new press. He also wanted a new set

---

[136] From *Sahibs and munshis*, p. 97.

[137] Ibid., p. 98.

Persian types to be made by the best artists in Calcutta, under the guidance of Sheikh Kutb Ali, the Persian writing master at the College. He argued that "the letters of the Persian alphabet are joined together in such a manner as to render the frequent use of Logographic types indispensably necessary to the accurate execution of any literary work that may be printed in the Persian character."[138] The types that were used by the College were meant to "imitate more nearly the written character" and it was hoped that the printed texts would vie with "manuscripts in beauty and cheapness" even as they surpassed manuscripts in "accuracy."[139] The types were executed under the immediate supervision of natives attached to the College.[140]

It is not surprising that there are detailed discussions on the painstaking efforts taken to create the new types of Indian languages, and the sheer beauty of these native mechanical fonts. The emphasis was on the mechanical superiority of print versus handwritten manuscripts and to understand the logic of this argument, one needs to remember that by the end of the eighteenth century, when the socio-cultural characteristics of print were carried alongside the technology of print itself, print culture was seen at the apex of the communication circuit in Europe. Print technology in Europe during the fifteenth and sixteenth centuries reflected the larger social shift that was

---

[138] Ibid., p. 99.

[139] *Annals*, p. 210.

[140] Ibid., p. 211.

taking place whereby handicraft productions were giving way to mechanical processes and scribes were being replaced.[141] For this change to occur, a fundamental shift had to take place where printed books were construed as more credible than manuscripts; printers thus started to champion the superior accuracy and credibility of books in comparison to manuscripts at the beginning of the sixteenth century.[142] There was nothing intrinsic to the trustworthiness of books, and in fact, Adrian Johns argues that when printed books were first published in the early modern period, textual corruptions multiplied but this time period also saw the social constructedness of printed texts as being fixed and credible in comparison to handwritten texts.[143]

Within the colonial context in Calcutta, when we look closely at the debates and rationale raised on how the realm of print was to emerge, the concerns were not merely with replacing a manuscript culture, but there was an equally strong emphasis on how beautiful the natives types were. Halhed, in the "Introduction" to the *Grammar of the Bengal Language* wrote on the mechanical aspects of the fonts:

> The public curiosity must be strongly excited by the beautiful characters which are displayed in the

---

[141] Eisenstein, 1979: 50-51, 54-55; McLuhan, 1994: 174.

[142] Johns, 1998, p. 5.

[143] Ibid., p.31.

following work: and although my attempt may be deemed incompleat or unworthy of notice, the book itself will always bear an intrinsic value, from its containing as extraordinary an influence of mechanic abilities as has perhaps ever appeared. That the Bengal letter is very difficult to be imitated in steel will readily be allowed by every person who shall examine the intricacies of the strokes, the unequal length and size of the characters, and the variety of their positions and combinations. It was no easy task to procure a writer accurate enough to prepare an alphabet of a similar and proportionate body throughout, and with that symmetrical exactness which is necessary to the regularity and neatness of a fount.[144]

The element of beauty involved in the creation of the types in Indian languages is a factor that has never been considered in how print was construed in Europe. In many ways, such a perspective compels us to be more nuanced in how empire worked in the colonial context, legitimizing the need to invest time, labour, money and people in establishing a realm of print.

Bakhtin: making sense of heteroglossia.

The heteroglossic newspaper that emerged, thus, was a pastiche of sorts – and in this particular context, more so as

---

[144] Halhed, p. xxiii.

a single news item was printed in multiple languages simultaneously on the same page. This heteroglossic text reveals a particular moment in the initial moments of colonial presence in Calcutta, and in many ways, reflects the multilingual nature of Indian society. To understand this phenomenon more comprehensively, Mikhail Bakhtin's notion of heteroglossia in a novel is quite pertinent.[145] Bakhtin writes that at any given moment of its evolution, language is stratified" into linguistic dialects but also into "languages that are socio-ideological: languages of social groups" and therefore, "literary language [used in novels] itself is only one of these heteroglot languages."[146] Language, therefore, is a reflection of society. In describing the heteroglossic novel, he writes at lengths about the nature of heteroglot languages:

> The novel as a whole is a phenomenon multiform in style and variform in speech and voice. In it the investigator is confronted with several heterogeneous stylistic unities, often located on different linguistic levels and subject to different stylistic controls.
> ...[T]hese heterogeneous stylistic unities, upon

[145] Mikhail Bakhtin, *The Dialogic Imagination*, edited by Michael Holquist (Austin: University of Texas Press, 2004). He describes it: "Heteroglossia, once incorporated into the novel ... is another's speech in another's language, serving to express authorial intentions but in a refracted way. Such speech constitutes a special type of double-voiced discourse. It serves two speakers at the same time and expresses simultaneously two different intentions... And all the while these two voices are dialogically interrelated, they... know about each other... it is as if they actually hold a conversation with each other." p. 324.

[146] Ibid., p. 272.

entering the novel, combine to form a structured artistic system, and are subordinated to the higher stylistic unity of the work as a whole, a unity that cannot be identified with any single one of the unities subordinated to it.

The novel orchestrates all its themes, the totality of the world of objects and ideas depicted and expressed in it, by means of the social diversity of speech types and by the differing individual voices that flourish under such conditions.[147]

Bakhtin urges us to go beyond the usual interpretative models of "linguistic and stylistic thought" that are used to understand the questions regarding the "philosophy of discourse."[148] There is an equation that he draws between society and language, and argues that that we must understand that the "life and behavior of discourse" reflects and emerges from a "contradictory and multi languaged world."[149] He goes on to write:

> The living utterance, having taken meaning and shape at a particular historical moment in a socially specific environment, cannot fail to brush up against thousands of living dialogic threads, woven by socio-ideological consciousness around the given object of an utterance; it cannot fail to become an active

---

[147] Ibid., pp. 261-263.

[148] Ibid., p. 275.

[149] Ibid., p. 275.

participant in social dialogue.[150]

It is reductive to look at language outside its social matrix and for Bakhtin, at any "given historical moment of verbal-ideological life," each generation has its own language, and therefore, "at any given moment, languages of various epochs and periods of socio-ideological life cohabit with one another."[151] The heteroglot nature of language represents the "co-existence of socio-ideological contradictions between the present and the past, between differing epochs of the past, between different socio-ideological groups in the present."[152] This coexistence of different linguistic styles and languages is an example of hybridization; which is a mixture of two social languages within the limits of a single utterance.[153]

The multilingual newspaper allowed the convergence of multiple languages that had and existed in different social moments in the history of India: English was the language of the new British rulers, while Persian had been used earlier and Bengali was the language in use by the inhabitants of Bengal. The hegemonic present of colonial rule, the native present and the immediate past all featured in this heteroglot text, creating the illusion of linguistic parity while in reality that was not the case. Examining the

---

[150] Ibid., p. 276.

[151] Ibid., p. 290-291.

[152] Ibid., p. 291.

[153] Ibid., p. 358.

reasons as to why such a multilingual text would exist does give us an opportunity to understand the heterogeneous nature of Indian society.

Section II.

COLLATED MANUSCRIPTS OF THE HINDU *SHASTRAS*.

Manuscripts of the Hindu religious texts were often transferred onto print in the early years of print culture in colonial Bengal, India, (i.e. during the last decades of the eighteenth century) under the aegis of the East India Company sponsored Orientalists, but what exactly were the processes involved? How did native-brahmins look upon it as they assisted the Britishers in making the shift take place from a manuscript culture to a realm of print technology?

In 1825, Graves Chamney Haughton, a professor of Hindu Literature in the East India College, published an out-of-print text, William Jones's translation of the Sanskrit

Manava Dharma Shastra or the *Institutes of Manu*.[154] Sir William Jones, an employee of the East India Company and referred to as the father of scientific linguistics and comparative philology, is a perfect example of a scholar who worked outside the Orientalist knowledge-making framework. He was also steeped in the culture of eighteenth century British print and had an immense trust in the veracity of printed texts. Haughton's prefatory note states that it was a new edition of Sir William Jones's translation; he writes that in his own text "the version of the learned translator has been carefully revised and compared" and that discrepancies would have been a result of the "variety of the manuscripts consulted by Sir William Jones." This observation provides us with historical documentation that there existed a "variety" of manuscripts that were consulted by these Orientalist scholars as they wrote their versions of the *Manusmriti*.

In 1794, the British government of India had Jones's *Manava Dharma* printed; Sir William Jones, writes in his preface about the processes involved in collaborating with the Brahmins in writing the text:

> …[A]nd the brahman, who read it with me, requested

---

[154] Throughout, I will be referring to *Manusmriti* and *Manavadharma*, synonymously. I will be using the following text: *Manavadharmasastra, or, The Institutes of Manu*, according to the Gloss of Kulluka, comprising the Indian system of Duties, Religious and Civil. Verbally translated from the original, with a Preface by Sir William Jones, and Collated with the Sanskrit Text, by Graves Chanmey Haughton, Esq., Professor of Hindu Literature in the East India College. THIRD EDITION, edited by The Revd. P. Percival, Professor of Vernacular Literature, Presidency College, Madras. (Madras, J. Higginbotham: 1863).

most earnestly, that his name might be concealed; nor would he have read it for any consideration on a forbidden day of the moon,… so great, indeed, is the idea of sanctity annexed to this book, that, when the chief magistrate at Benaras endeavoured, at my request, to procure a Persian translation of it, before I had a hope of being at any time able to understand the original, the Pandits of his court unanimously and positively refused to assist in the work; nor should I have procured it at all, if a wealthy Hindu at Gaya had not caused the version to be made by some of his dependants.

The question to ask is thus: did natives operate within a different parallel epistemic world where multiple manuscripts of the same text were seen as legitimate; moreover, why were the brahmins not necessarily keen to see their names on print, but neither were they hesitant to transfer a manuscript culture onto print? These early decades of colonial print can throw more light on the nature of religious-manuscripts that existed in India, before the advent of print in India. More importantly and is of relevance, is that: when we read a text like *Manusmriti*, why exactly should we assume that there exists an intact, untouched, version of the text?

Till as recently as two hundred years ago, India was a manuscript culture meaning that the printed text did not exist. When the transition took place from a manuscript culture to a print one, it seems to have taken place easelessly, implying that the shift was made without much murmurs and complaints from at least the native, elite sections of society. The Britishers, on the other hand, at seeing the beautiful manuscripts in Indian languages, must have been reminded of their pre-print past and a lot of care was taken to ensure that these manuscripts were well kept. When Tipu Sultan lost the Mysore wars (1780-90s), his library was also taken and a concern was raised by the Company soldiers as to how the manuscripts were to be kept safe: "That part of the library of the late Tippoo Sultan, which was presented by the army to the Court of Directors, is lately arrived in Bengal; the Governor-General strongly recommends that the Oriental manuscripts composing this collection, should be deposited in the library of the College of Fort William, and it is his intention to retain the manuscripts accordingly, until he shall receive the orders of the Court upon the subject."[155] There was no rampant erasure of the Indian manuscript past, and in fact, the Company was keen to preserve this aspect of Indian

---

[155] *The Annals of the College of Fort William, from the Period of its Foundation.*Arranged and Published by Thomas Roebuck, Calcutta, Printed by Philip Periera at the Hindoostanee Press, 1819. "Introduction" pp. xxv. The report mentions the importance of preserving old manuscripts: "The preservation and augmentation of the Collection of Eastern Manuscripts, afford the only means of arresting the progressive destruction of Oriental learning. Since the dismemberment of the Muslim, those works have been dispersed over India, and have been exposed to the injuries and hazards of time, accident and neglect. It is worthy of the ambition of this great Empire to employ every effort of its influence in preserving from destruction and decay, these valuable records of Oriental history, Science and Religion." p. 114.

culture.

The larger question, though, is: can we ever take it for a given that what we know, in a definitive manner, as being central to the Hindu *shastras* can be construed as being infallible? - for all we know – these texts might have been amended and changes made as they were handed down generations. In the preface to his version of *Manavadharma*, Sir William Jones wrote about the textual variations that existed and how he collated different versions that were available in manuscript form to arrive at his final text:[156]

> At length appeared KULLU'KA BHATTA; who, after a painful course of study and the collation of numerous manuscripts, produced a work, of which it may, perhaps, be said very truly, that it is the shortest, yet the most luminous, the least ostentatious, yet the most learned, the deepest, yet the most agreeable, commentary ever composed on any author [namely, Manu] ancient or modern, European or Asiatic. The Pandits care so little for genuine chronology, that none of them can tell me the age of KULLU'KA, whom they always name with applause; but he informs us himself, that he was a *Brahmin* of the *Varéndra* tribe, whose family had been long settled in *Gaur* or Bengal, but that he

---

[156] Ibid.

had chosen his residence among the learned on the banks of the holy river at Ka'si. His text and interpretation I have almost implicitly followed, though I had myself collated many copies of MANU, and among them a manuscript of a very ancient date: …

We can arrive at the obvious conclusion that William Jones consulted many textual variations of the *Manusmriti*, and if so, the implication is that there was no single authoritative text. If these texts that constitute our Hindu *shastras* are unreliable with numerous variants existing simultaneously, then it stands to reason that there is no authentic version that we can refer to as being the original. Who is to tell as to which part comprised "revealed knowledge" and which sections were subsequent add-ons?

WORKING NOTES

www.ingramcontent.com/pod-product-compliance
Lightning Source LLC
Chambersburg PA
CBHW070638030426
42337CB00020B/4073